The Letort Papers

DECIDING TO BUY:
CIVIL-MILITARY RELATIONS
AND MAJOR WEAPONS PROGRAMS

Quentin E. Hodgson

November 2010

*****

Comments pertaining to this report are invited and should be forwarded to: Director, Strategic Studies Institute, U.S. Army War College, 122 Forbes Ave, Carlisle, PA 17013-5244.

*****

A project of even these modest proportions benefits from the insight, thought, and encouragement of many others than just the author. While the errors that survive are mine alone, it was not for lack of help from many others. In particular, I would like to thank Dr. Joseph Collins and Mr. Tim Morgan for their guidance, encouragement, and enthusiasm throughout this process. Mr. John Matheny helped point me towards the B-1 as a case study and encouraged me to pursue the research. My thanks to Dr. Stephen Randolph for his assistance in understanding some of the more byzantine workings of archives. Thank you to the wonderful staff at the National Defense University Library, particularly Jose Torres for his help with congressional records and Pamela Stroh for finding the needle in a haystack. I thank Dave Des Roches for his thoughtful guidance during a chance encounter on the Washington Metro. My thanks as well to Dr. Todd Kauderer for his deep knowledge of naval history. The staff at the National Archives in College Park, Maryland, was helpful and patient in guiding me through the collection, particularly the reading room and classified reading room staffs. I hope that file turns up one day.

This paper is dedicated to Leslie for her love, encouragement, and patience. The clutter will disappear eventually, I swear.

*****

All Strategic Studies Institute (SSI) publications may be downloaded free of charge from the SSI website. Hard copies of this report may also be obtained free of charge by placing an order on the SSI website. The SSI website address is: *www.StrategicStudiesInstitute.army.mil.*

*****

The Strategic Studies Institute publishes a monthly e-mail newsletter to update the national security community on the research of our analysts, recent and forthcoming publications, and upcoming conferences sponsored by the Institute. Each newsletter also provides a strategic commentary by one of our research analysts. If you are interested in receiving this newsletter, please subscribe on the SSI website at *www.StrategicStudiesInstitute. army.mil/newsletter/.*

ISBN 1-58487-467-8

FOREWORD

The wars in Afghanistan and Iraq have brought to public attention a number of issues concerning the role of the civilian leadership in the Department of Defense (DoD) and the military. Although popular writings have focused on the alleged failings of DoD leadership from former Secretary of Defense Donald Rumsfeld on down, there is a much longer running dispute between the civilians and military in the Pentagon. This dispute centers on how money is allocated across the Department and where funds should be invested. As we draw down in Iraq and look towards setting Afghanistan on a sustainable path to stability and self-governance, the DoD will have to contend with a constricting fiscal environment, the need to recapitalize equipment, reset and reconstitute units, and prepare for a future security environment that holds many challenges for the United States, its partners, and allies. To address these future challenges, the Services will want to harness the latest technologies and continue modernization and transformation, including examining requirements for next-generation aircraft, ships, and land combat systems.

In this timely monograph, Mr. Quentin Hodgson explores how the civilian and military leadership of the Pentagon have debated and argued decisions on major weapons programs. Drawing on interviews with participants and archival research, he has demonstrated the enduring nature of these debates, despite efforts to improve, transform, and overhaul the defense planning and programming system. Starting with the advent of the Department's planning and programming system under Secretary of Defense Robert McNamara in the 1960s, Mr. Hodgson traces the evolving debate over the role of nuclear propulsion in surface ships for the Navy, including the changing perspectives on the roles of analysis versus military judgment. He highlights that these debates are not exclusive to one Service by examining the dialogue across administrations between the Air Force and the political leadership that culminated in the cancellation, and later resurrection, of the B-1 bomber. Finally, he looks at one of the most prevalent and public debates of recent memory between the Army and Secretary Rumsfeld over the development of the Crusader artillery system. In each case, he has rightly included the role of Congress as a critical component.

Mr. Hodgson's lessons learned in his conclusion are a healthy reminder that miracle cures are unlikely to resolve these sources of conflict, and in many respects these tensions are necessary and desirable when the impacts of the decisions can be momentous. I commend his work to civilian and military leaders alike.

DOUGLAS C. LOVELACE, JR.
Director
Strategic Studies Institute

ABOUT THE AUTHOR

QUENTIN E. HODGSON is a strategist in the Office of the Secretary of Defense (OSD). He was a strategic planner in OSD, where he was the primary author of the 2008 National Defense Strategy and supported the Secretary of Defense and Under Secretary of Defense for Policy in providing guidance for and reviews of combatant command contingency plans. He previously worked in the Stability Operations office in OSD, where he devised and implemented new policies to increase military capabilities to conduct stability operations, counterinsurgency, and peacekeeping. Mr. Hodgson was the Department of Defense lead on the President's Global Peace Operations Initiative, a multiyear program with G-8 partners to increase peacekeeping capabilities worldwide. He joined OSD in 2001 as a Presidential Management Intern, completing planning rotations in OSD Policy and at U.S. Pacific Command, as well as working on the Southeast Asia and Russia desks. Mr. Hodgson is an associate member of the International Institute for Strategic Studies and a member of the Society for Military History. His research interests include Thomas Jefferson's political thought and civil-military relations. Mr. Hodgson holds a B.A. in history and Russian from the Johns Hopkins University, and an M.A. in international relations, specializing in strategic studies and international economics, from the Paul H. Nitze School of Advanced International Studies. He was a Fulbright Scholar at the University of Potsdam and studied at the School of Slavonic and East European Studies in London. He is a 2009 graduate of the Industrial College of the Armed Forces.

SUMMARY

The development and procurement of major weapons programs in the United States is a complex and often drawn-out process complicated by political considerations and often sharp disagreements over requirements and the merits of systems. Secretaries of Defense since Robert McNamara have sought to impose discipline on the process, with varying degrees of success. Conflicts between a military service and the civilian leadership are inevitable. A Service wants to develop the most advanced system to address its perceived need, whereas the Secretary of Defense must balance competing requirements across the Department of Defense. The military and the civilian leadership may also have different strategic perspectives that feed this conflict. Through the detailed analysis of three case studies — the Nuclear Surface Navy in the 1960s, the B-1 Bomber in the 1970s, and the Crusader artillery system in the 2000s — the author explores some of the common themes and sources of friction that arise in civil-military relations concerning major weapons programs. He concludes with some thoughts on how the Secretary of Defense can anticipate and reduce these sources of friction, while retaining an environment that supports healthy debate.

DECIDING TO BUY:
CIVIL-MILITARY RELATIONS
AND MAJOR WEAPONS PROGRAMS

INTRODUCTION

The history of the Office of the Secretary of Defense (OSD), since its inception, is also the history of the development of capabilities necessary to control and implement strategy in the Department of Defense (DoD). James Forrestal, who served as the first Secretary of Defense (SecDef), recognized that the SecDef needed more power to impose discipline on the military services. Since then OSD has sought to implement greater control while the Services have fought to maintain their independence. The Defense Act of 1958 gave the SecDef control over the allocation of resources among the Services for the first time, effectively transforming him from a mere arbiter into a decisionmaker. However, it was not until the SecDef decided to exercise this new authority and implement the management processes to facilitate it, that we saw the emergence of the SecDef office as we recognize it today. Robert McNamara was not the first to have these powers, but he served long enough, had the support of the President, and also possessed enough willpower to grapple with the issues while also attempting to impose discipline in the process.

Civil-military relations have a rich tradition of study in American scholarship.[1] Samuel Huntington's seminal work, *The Soldier and the State*, serves as the basis of modern scholarship on the subject, even for those who challenge his theory of civil-military relations. One aspect of Huntington's book is of particular importance for this paper: Huntington pointed out the

1

unique nature of the profession of arms and the expertise required in building and employing military forces for the purposes of organized destruction;[2] or, as Harold Lasswell would call it, the "management of violence."[3] The martial profession has developed steadily over the course of history, but industrialization and increasingly technological means of destruction and killing have led to the profession of arms being characterized as much by technical expertise as by Carl von Clausewitz's *coup d'oeil*.[4]

This technological development has led to a growing need to fully understand the technology of war, not just the passions of war. What are the soldiers' tools, and how are they used? This is a critical question that militaries, particularly Western ones, have wrestled with and to which they have often drawn the wrong conclusions, but always moving forward towards increasing destructiveness and ferocity. Soldiers no longer bring their weapons to battle from the farmstead or the baronial estate; the state has taken on the responsibility of arming and often caring for and feeding the soldier, even in times of peace. In the United States and various other nations, this has given rise to vast bureaucracies responsible for creating a budget for and managing such programs.

This model gives rise to inevitable conflicts when ministries and departments run by civilians seek to impose restrictions on the relatively high-cost military and aforementioned military programs. In some cases, the same civilians have previously served in the military, but often they have not.[5] The latter group's understanding of the needs of the military varies with each individual, but it, unfortunately, often conflicts with the military services' perception of their own needs. Though much scholarship has focused

2

on times of apparent civil-military crisis—episodes such as Truman's firing of Douglas MacArthur during the Korean War; the dereliction of duty of the Joint Chiefs of Staff during the Vietnam War; and the public disagreements between Army Chief of Staff Eric Shinseki and Deputy Secretary of Defense Paul Wolfowitz about the troop numbers required for the 2003 invasion of Iraq—this brand of conflict occurs during times of peace as well, often with far-reaching impacts that the various participants cannot even fathom at the time the dispute takes place. Civil-military relations are about more than how to conduct oneself during war and decisions about going to war.

Defense strategy plays out in many arenas. Which conflicts the military will engage in and the methods it will employ during said conflicts are obviously important aspects, as are the types of equipment the military will need and how it will acquire the equipment. Visions of future warfare often differ, and can be either near-psychic in nature or catastrophically wrong, as the French discovered in World War II.[6] What a military buys defines, in many respects, how it fights. Thus the decision about which capabilities to acquire is of supreme importance. It revolves not just around whether or not to buy, but also how many, and of what type. For example, by 1943 Soviet armored units in World War II were organized around a limited number of vehicles (particularly the T-34 tank), whereas German armored units often encompassed a dozen types of armored vehicles of varying complexity.[7]

This paper's central focus will be on three case studies which will answer the question of how senior civilian leaders in the DoD and the White House arrive at decisions on what to buy, and how they implement those decisions, particularly when the affected military department has different opinions on what should be bought. This paper does not seek to answer the question of who is right and who is wrong, but rather to look at how those charged with controlling the military come into conflict with the military and how they resolve issues related to the decisions that affect the potential course of future conflicts.

These case studies are not intended to provide universally applicable lessons, though there are remarkably consistent features in all of them. This is primarily an historical analysis (as opposed to a work of political science) to delve deeply into the cases, identify the arguments on both sides, isolate the actors, and explain the cases' individual outcomes. From these cases, some preliminary conclusions about the nature of decisionmaking and of major weapons programs will be drawn, which, it is hoped, will provide insight into how to improve future approaches.

These case studies cover a relatively long period, but demonstrate some constants, such as the role of Congress, the conflict over information, and differing levels of analysis. In some cases, one could easily use a quotation from an actor in 2002 in the context of the 1960s, and it would not seem out of place.[8] Care has been taken to choose cases that have had an impact on each of the three main military branches, the Army, Navy, and Air Force, to show there are no particular biases or peculiarities in the relations between any one branch and the civilian leadership. The case studies are also exemplifications of their time periods. It may appear these cases have been chosen because they are sensational examples, but the richest case studies often result from the greatest conflicts. The dynamics were no different in the following studies than in other cases, just a bit more conspicuous. The cases have also been chosen because they occurred during both Democratic and Republican administrations. This should control for any biases which may result from a particular party's approach to civil-military relations.

Finally, the first two case studies occurred against the backdrop of the Cold War. The last case study occurred at the outset of a newer conflict with a new nature that we are still adjusting to at the time of this writing (Spring 2009), but which has only had a marginal impact on the debate. There were irregular challenges in each of the three cases, against which the government was forced to test the viability of whatever new weapon system was under consideration at the time.

THE NUCLEAR NAVY

This analysis begins with the origins of the modern DoD system used for devising, analyzing, and budgeting for military requirements. The first case study highlights the difference in opinion between the military branches and the senior civilian leadership in DoD. On this occasion, the Navy took the position that whatever could improve tactical and operational capabilities was worthy of pursuit. However, in order to deal with the civilian leadership, the SecDef in particular, in a seemingly more sophisticated, less emotive manner, the Navy gradually and grudgingly adopted a more rigorously analytical approach toward deciding which capabilities were necessary. The following case study provides an excellent example of how assumptions, perspective, costs, Congress, and comparative arguments can each play a critical role in determining what the DoD decides to buy and how it arrives at said decisions.

Robert McNamara and the Advent of Systems Analysis.

Robert Strange McNamara had barely been named head of the Ford Corporation in 1960 when newly elected President John F. Kennedy asked him to become the new SecDef. McNamara had served in the Army Air Corps during World War II, mainly in the Office of Statistical Control, and since the end of the war he had been one of a group of "Whiz Kids"[9] recruited into Ford Motor Corporation whose goal was to help revive the company. He used his background in systems analysis and business studies at Harvard to bring a more active form of management to the DoD in 1961.

Although the position of SecDef was less than 2 decades old at that point, McNamara already had eight predecessors who had tried, with varying degrees of success, to implement change and manage the vast competing bureaucracies which made up the military-branch departments. Forrestal had vigorously opposed the creation of the office when he was Secretary of the Navy (SECNAV), but after a few months as Truman's SecDef, he realized the weak powers of the office needed bolstering.[10] Although the National Security Act of 1947 gave the SecDef nominal supremacy in the department, it took several attempts to properly rectify the shortcomings of the office. These attempts included an amendment in 1949 that demoted the Service secretaries from cabinet-level positions; and, more importantly, the Defense Reorganization Act of 1958, which strengthened the SecDef's office and created the position of Director of Defense Research and Engineering (DDR&E), among other endeavors.

SecDef Neil McElroy, the first beneficiary of the 1958 Act, did not have much time to fully implement the measures for which the Act called, and he largely allowed the Services to continue to set priorities within their respective budgets.[11]

McNamara recognized that the department needed new management tools to control the burgeoning defense budget. As Alain Enthoven termed it, the defense budget prior to the Kennedy administration "was far from the vital policy instrument it should have been. Rather than a mechanism for integrating strategy, forces, and costs, it was essentially a bookkeeping device for dividing funds between services and accounts and a blunt instrument for keeping a lid on defense spending."[12] McNamara's Planning-Programming-Budgeting System (PPBS) of 1962 sought to tie a program to clearly articulated strategic goals, provide a means to examine alternatives, and establish clear criteria for judging the relative merits of competing programs.[13] The system was intended to raise the decisionmaking on acquisitions and procurement to the highest levels, but also allow all the players in the process to see the costs over the long term and balance those costs against military requirements. Another forecasted benefit was PPBS's transition from a 1-year budget projection to a multiyear focus that was intended to result in more specific discussions of Out-Year Costs.[14]

The original 5-Year Defense Plan (FYDP) covered 10 major military programs (strategic forces, general-purpose forces, intelligence and communications, airlift and sealift, guard and reserve forces, research and development, central supply and maintenance, training and medical services, administration and associated activities, and support to other nations) and showed an 8-year projection of forces alongside a 5-year projection of costs and manpower.[15] McNamara, Assistant Secretary of Defense Charlie Hitch, and Director for Weapons Systems Analysis Enthoven hoped to engage the military services in an open debate on future requirements. Although it did not seem so at the time to many military officers, it was also designed to give the Service chiefs a greater say in the budget. Prior to 1961, the Joint Chiefs of Staff were not asked for their opinion on the budget; through the Draft Presidential Memorandum on the defense budget, they were given an opportunity to comment.[16]

However, for the first time the SecDef and his civilian subordinates were also not just giving a top-line budget to the military departments. They were pushing and prodding to understand the reasoning behind the military's choices and challenging the conclusions the different branches came to, particularly by challenging the oft-unspoken assumptions upon which decisions were made. Enthoven wrote in his seminal work, *How Much is Enough*, that analysis relies critically on assumptions, and since assumptions can be challenged, analysis should never be accepted as universally "correct."[17] This belief was too much for officers who believed the military, by virtue of its operational experience, had the monopoly on the correct answers. General Thomas D. White, former Air Force Chief of Staff made the point clearly in 1963 when he said:

> In common with many other military men, active and retired, I am profoundly apprehensive of the pipe-smoking, tree-full-of-owls type of so-called professional 'defense intellectuals' who have been brought into this nation's capitol. I don't believe a lot of these often over-confident, sometimes arrogant young professors, mathematicians and other theorists have suffi-

cient worldliness or motivation to stand up to the kind of enemy we face.[18]

Vice Admiral Hyman Rickover was also a critic of civilian force planners, and, in May 1968, called them all "spiritualists" and "sociologists" and accused them of "playing at God while neglecting the responsibility of being human."[19] Naturally, any change to the status quo stimulates opposition, but in this case the source of the conflict was deeper. The civilian analysts were challenging the heretofore uncontested military domination over defense investment choices.

McNamara's First Budget Moves.

Every new administration faces a daunting task when it first arrives in office: adjusting priorities in the budget. The incoming administration will work for almost its entire first year under a budget that was developed and submitted by the outgoing administration and passed by the previous year's Congress. The first elements of change in the budget only come with a revised submission of the budget for the fiscal year, which starts on October 1 of the administration's first year. Although a presidential candidate will have made numerous pledges during the campaign regarding spending priorities and programs, he is still faced with combing through a massive budget submission to implement any changes once he makes it into office. McNamara decided to tackle the problem by examining the big programs in the budget and creating a draft memorandum for the President outlining his recommendations for changes to the budget.[20]

Assistant Secretary of Defense Hitch distributed a top secret memo to the Joint Chiefs of Staff in early February along with a draft of the memo McNamara intended to send to the President in late February. In the memo, McNamara noted that he had reviewed the Dwight Eisenhower administration's Fiscal Year (FY) 1961 and FY 1962 budgets based on his understanding of each year's national security objectives, and with the help and advice of Secretary of State Dean Rusk and other members of the White House staff.[21] He noted further that:

> The task of thinking through the implications of national security objectives for military force structure is a tremendously complex and necessarily a continuing one. This review of the current budget has been able to deal with only the most urgent and obvious problems. Existing analyses on some of the central issues of general nuclear war made it possible to penetrate most deeply into this area. However, here, as with limited war, much more study is required, and will be undertaken as a matter of urgency before the FY 1963 budget is presented.[22]

Two major components of the message, the issue of nuclear propulsion for the Navy and the B-70 bomber, will be addressed below.

By 1961, the Navy had demonstrated the ability to provide nuclear propulsion in submarines. The Atomic Energy Commission (AEC), which jointly controlled the development of nuclear reactors along with the DoD, was constantly looking for new opportunities to push the use of nuclear power. In its task, the AEC was aided by Admiral Hyman Rickover, recognized by many as the father of the nuclear navy. The problem was that nuclear-powered ships were extremely expensive to build. USS *Enterprise* was the first nuclear-powered carrier; it was commissioned in November 1961 at a cost of nearly $500 million dollars, but it had not demonstrated full capabilities yet.[23]

The question also remained about how far to extend nuclear propulsion. An aircraft carrier does not travel alone but in a task force with support ships and other capital ships. Because of this, would all the ships in the task force need to be nuclear-powered for the military to take advantage of the full benefits of nuclear propulsion? In such a case, the costs would be staggering.[24] A nuclear-powered submarine had obvious advantages over its conventionally-powered cousins. It could stay submerged for much longer periods of time, was quieter while running its engines, and was faster than any diesel-powered submarine. Surface ships, on the other hand, were more costly to build, man, operate, and maintain than oil-powered ships.[25] Whether these costs were justified by increased performance would remain a hotly contested issue for much of the 1960s.

Initially the Navy was not a fierce advocate of nuclear propulsion for surface ships, though there was an interest in seeing how much, if at all, it could benefit the Navy. Admiral Arleigh Burke, who served as Chief of Naval Operations (CNO) from 1955 to 1961, revealed his vision of a Navy consisting of 927 ships, with 6 all-nuclear carrier task forces, by the beginning of the 1970s. But even he recognized that rising costs could kill his dreams of such a fleet while they were still on the drawing board.[26] In 1960, Secretary of the Navy Thomas S. Gates testified before Congress that the Navy was requesting authorization and funding to build a non-nuclear-powered carrier because the increased costs of nuclear propulsion would not be offset, in his opinion, by increased steaming capacity.[27] After the construction of the first nuclear carrier, the Navy was unsure it wanted to proceed with a second one until as late as 1962.[28]

McNamara was inclined to agree with former Secretary of the Navy Gates. He was primarily concerned with the costs of providing fully nuclear task forces. Although the main debate in the first Kennedy budget centered on the carrier (designated CVA-67), the costs associated with the accompanying ships played a large role as well. Admiral Burke's vision for the end of the decade had involved a task force with an aircraft carrier, two guided missile cruisers, and three frigates, all with nuclear propulsion.[29]

McNamara's advisors looked at several alternatives for nuclear propulsion and its role in the surface navy, including the possibility of completely converting all the carriers, cruisers, and frigates — the main components of an attack carrier task force — to nuclear power. They conceded that "tactical flexibility is considerably enhanced by nuclear propulsion,"[30] especially since it removed the need to conserve fuel. They estimated that a carrier steaming at 20 knots had a designed endurance of 8,000 miles (which would be just enough to steam from Hawaii to the China Sea and back) with conventional power, but could reach an astounding 475,000 miles with nuclear power. A carrier by itself could maintain high rates of speed for extended periods of time in order to get to the area of operations quickly, but it would still need support ships that could keep up with it.[31]

The nuclear-powered cruisers and frigates did not quite have the designed endurance of the carriers, but the frigates were quite close. OSD analysts noted that these advantages dissipated if not all the support ships were nuclear-powered, and that the ships would still be needed to resupply the carriers with food, aviation fuel, and ammunition, among other things. However, larger ships, generally nuclear-powered vessels, did not afford significantly more storage space to stock more of these supplies. On the other hand, a conventionally-powered carrier's endurance was roughly equal to its utilization rate for other supplies in a cold war environment.[32] In other words, it had enough fuel to last, in most cases, until such time that even a nuclear-powered carrier would have to take on supplies anyway.

Given these limitations, it seemed that the relative cost difference between conventional and nuclear-powered systems seemed to favor those who were against switching to nuclear power. However, OSD analysts noted that building three aircraft carriers and nine frigates with nuclear power would add $642 million to the 5-Year Defense Program, enough money to add another two conventional carriers, or seven guided missile frigates (DLG), and operate them for 20 years.[33] The analysts stated that, in some cases, having ships use nuclear power to get to various hot spots around the world was a desirable prospect, but they also recommended against outfitting more than one carrier group with nuclear-powered propulsion at the time, given constraints on the budget in other areas.

Introducing the Planning, Programming, Budgeting System.

The FY63 budget was the first full budget to institute the Planning, Programming, Budgeting System (PPBS).[34] Prior to the implementation of PPBS, the different military branches had constructed their budgets independently, with little interference from the SecDef or the Bureau of Budget (now the Office of Management and Budget [OMB]), except to abide by the budget ceilings set by those offices. With the previous budget system, each branch was able to build its budget based on its own needs, but they usually did so without regard for the capabilities of the other branches. Former Army Chief of Staff General Maxwell Taylor summarized the issue in his congressional testimony in 1960:

> In spite of the fact that modern war is no longer fought in terms of separate Army, Navy, and Air Force, nonetheless we still budget vertically in these service terms. Yet, if we are called upon to fight, we will not be interested in the services as such. We will be interested rather in task forces, these combinations of Army, Navy, and Air Force which are functional in nature, such as the atomic retaliatory forces, overseas deployments, continental air defense forces, limited war expeditionary forces, and the like. But the point is that we do not keep our budget in these terms. Hence it is not an exaggeration to say that we do not know what kind and how much defense we are buying with any specific budget.[35]

McNamara planned to amend this situation and, in accordance with his charges from President Kennedy, procure the best force possible at the lowest possible cost. Hitch and Enthoven, among others, thought it would be too ambitious to implement the PPBS changes all at once, and proposed starting only with strategic forces in the FY63 budget. McNamara insisted on applying the system to the entire defense program "in less than a year."[36] The main focus of PPBS was to provide decisionmakers in the Pentagon with continuous updates and input during the entire budget—and defense program—building process, instead of the typical once-a-year inputs they gave as the budget came together. The budget was broken into sections, each detailing a certain major project. This gave the SecDef and others a broader view of capabilities development and how costs might build up or otherwise change over an extended period of time. This allowed for the examination of program choices at several points during their development, starting with their inception, and took away the need to wait for milestones further on in the developmental process.[37]

The FY63 budget also led to the initiation of a series of cost-effectiveness studies, which examined the capabilities of both proposed and established programs and compared them to one another based on their cost. This new system required the military to provide much more cost data than previously, and challenged their domination of systems expertise.[38] Despite the quick pace at which McNamara wished to implement the new system, Hitch was pleasantly surprised at the quality of data and analysis he received from the Services. Although some submissions, such as those from the general purpose forces, described the weapon systems and forces themselves rather than their effectiveness or potential effectiveness, the military branches as a whole adapted well to the changes.[39]

The FY64 Budget—Moving Forward on Nuclear Propulsion.

In the FY64 budget, which Hitch began constructing in the summer of 1962, McNamara requested that one naval task force be outfitted with nuclear-powered propulsion, but also called for the suspension of further nuclear shipbuilding while the costs and benefits of the nuclear-powered task force were reviewed.[40] The reviews were not based on cost alone, however. McNamara was concerned about the development of the *Typhon* frigate and its associated air defense system. The nuclear-powered *Typhon* (guided missile-nuclear [DLGN]) was a new frigate which provided greater defense for its fleet than previous models by combining missiles and an advanced radar system. In the FY64 budget, McNamara requested just one *Typhon* frigate with nuclear propulsion; he requested that any other frigates purchased be powered with conventional propulsion. He stated that further development of the nuclear guided missile frigate could continue in 1965. However, the purchase of the DLGN, which was supposed to take place in 1963, was pushed back 2 years while the funds originally designated for this were put toward other systems—more specifically, the Tartar, Terrier, and Talos air defense missile systems—which were already under construction.

Around the same time, McNamara testified that the destroyer force would shrink dramatically throughout the decade, and decline from the 207 ships it held in 1963 to 120 in 1971. He also determined that the guided missile escort ship (DEG) had "priced itself out of the program,"[41] since a DEG was estimated to cost $11 million more than a regular destroyer escort, over 25 percent more expensive.[42] This fact shows that McNamara's decisions about which capabilities to acquire were consistently based on price, as well as the capability's potential long-term value.

During the fall of 1962, there was much debate over possible revisions for the Navy shipbuilding program. In late October, Hitch prepared a draft of the memorandum for the President, which was then distributed for internal departmental review. The Navy wanted to maintain a sizable fleet of 852 ships and create a fairly large new-construction program that would last through the end of the decade. McNamara, on the other hand, believed it should buy fewer new ships—

he wanted to purchase 249 between FY63 and FY68, while the Navy had originally requested 322—and convert some of the old ships to make up part of the difference. Even with a larger number of conversions than primarily planned (94, as opposed to the Navy's initial request for 67), McNamara's program would yield 46 fewer new and converted ships at the end of the program period.[43] However, this was also more than he had sought in the previous year's budget.[44]

Based on the preliminary Navy analysis, Congress was primed to expect a much larger number of ships required than the number it officially received later. The Navy had told Congress earlier in 1962 that full modernization of the fleet by FY 1973 would require 366 new construction ships and 67 conversions in FY64-68, but later analysis showed that 68 of the ships that the Navy originally planned to replace could stay through the mid-1970s. As such, the Navy ended up scaling back the number of ships in its official request based on this analysis, but added a shipbuilding program in the FY63 budget, as well as a program McNamara deemed "highly tentative" because he had not had sufficient time to conduct a detailed analysis of it yet. Even so, McNamara approved the budget.

McNamara noted in his later testimony on the shipbuilding program, "with regard to fleet obsolescence, there has been a tendency to focus attention on the wrong set of facts. What we should be concerned with is not the chronological age of a particular ship, but whether it is able to perform its mission in the face of the expected threat, that is, whether it is tactically obsolescent." He went on to state his belief that "we are now all in agreement in the Pentagon that obsolescence based on age alone is not a useful concept."[45] In these comments, McNamara conveyed his belief that the Navy's budgetary appetite needed to be more controlled.

The Navy hardly agreed with McNamara, arguing in its November 9, 1962, memorandum to the SecDef that the fleet faced "block obsolescence" and that fully effective ships should comprise the force structure.[46] The memorandum for the President, which was truly aimed more at the DoD than the President himself, was McNamara's tool for explaining his view and trying to convince, or perhaps bludgeon, his opponents into submission. In a number of cases, he recommended putting off the construction of new ships meant to replace ships that had been in the fleet for years, since he was already dealing with the retirement of many World War II-era ships, and he wanted to avoid adding to his fiscal burden if at all possible. He was also wary of the apparent rush to field the new nuclear-powered ships, which, thus far, were still underdeveloped or untested technologies, hence his hesitation to support the Navy's request for four nuclear-powered *Typhon* destroyers (guided missile-nuclear destroyer [DDGN]). The Navy had requested a total of nine *Typhon* DDGNs over the FY65-68 time frame,[47] but the *Typhon* missile system had not been fully developed yet. Additionally, McNamara was awaiting a more concrete understanding of the capabilities of a single-reactor nuclear propulsion system, given that *Enterprise* had eight reactor plants, and no surface ship had yet put to sea with only one reactor.

The Navy asked for a nuclear-powered, missile-enabled frigate, the *Terrier* class, in the FY63 shipbuilding program, and for conventionally-powered *Typhon* frigates in FY64 through FY67. The Navy planned to set enough funding aside to construct one *Typhon* each year, except in FY66, in which it planned to build two.[48] In a November 1962 memo to McNamara, Hitch recommended going a less ambitious route and waiting to build the one nuclear-powered frigate in FY65 as previously planned, but he also offered McNamara some possible alternatives. One option involved constructing a conventionally-powered *Terrier* DLG in FY63 using the $70.5 million savings that would result in improved *Terrier*, *Tartar*, and *Talos* missile systems; this would increase the FY64 budget for shipbuilding by $25 million and roughly even out the costs over the next 4 years. A second option involved building the ship foreseen for FY67 in FY66, but the Navy would not be granted any of its other requests. Finally, the third option involved adding another *Typhon* to the program in FY66, while also granting the Navy's full request for six DLG frigates, but these requests would not be met according to the Navy's original schedule. In the margins of his copy of the memo, McNamara noted that the third alternative "would be my preference."[49]

The Navy's approach to gaining the nuclear-powered ships it wanted, when it wanted them, was interesting, to say the least. In October 1962, when OSD announced the cancellation of the *Terrier*-class frigate in FY63, and planned use of the nuclear-powered *Typhon* in FY65 in its place, the Navy submitted a "reclama" which aimed to pocket the *Typhon* and reinstate the *Terrier*-class frigate for the time being; despite the original Navy request for only one of the two ships, it now wanted both. The Navy argued that the preliminary OSD numbers would take the fleet from 852 to 828 total ships, below a comfortable level of total force structure effectiveness. Additionally, the Navy wanted a full nuclear-powered task force to go along with the FY63 guided-missile frigate, despite admitting that "the AAW [anti-aircraft warfare] capability of *Terrier* is . . . less than that expected of *Typhon*."[50] The Navy then stated that, as a result of this fact, waiting 2 years for the *Typhon* "would both lessen the effectiveness of the nuclear task force and unduly retard the further refinement of surface ship nuclear propulsion."[51] Finally, the Navy reminded the Secretary that Congress was expecting a nuclear-powered frigate in the FY63 budget.[52] Their approach to getting what they wanted was certainly not a subtle one.

The cost differential between the nuclear-propelled and conventionally-propelled ships was not insignificant. The FY63, nuclear-powered *Typhon*-class frigate would cost $190 million, while its conventionally-powered equivalent would cost 35 percent less, at only $123 million each. It is important to note that decisions over what capabilities to acquire were based primarily on the procurement cost, not total life-cycle cost. In the program reviews, the Navy argued that "as a result of a re-evaluation of the DLG [*Typhon*] program, the approved program has been decreased from 8 to 5 in recognition of the introduction of a guided missile single nuclear reactor destroyer (DDG(N)(TYPHON) which will provide a considerable increase in endurance and tactical flexibility."[53] It is unclear whether the Navy provided any additional analysis on the substance of this increased flexibility, but we know from McNamara's side of the debate over the FY63 aircraft carrier (the CVA-67) that he was dissatisfied with the Navy's supposed analysis of the increased flexibility and negligible cost differences.[54]

Marking Time—The FY65 Budget.

In 1963, McNamara sought to mark time on the nuclear propulsion question. He testified before the House Armed Services Committee on January 27, 1964, just 2 months after Kennedy's assassination, on the FY65 budget and 1965-69 defense program. This was his third full year working on the defense program—certainly enough time to feel comfortable with the budgeting process and to have begun to address major strategic issues. Despite this fact, he continued to call for more study of nuclear propulsion in surface warships. He ascribed the problems facing a nuclear navy to the development of more efficient and lighter reactors. Given the size and weight of the existing nuclear power sources, a nuclear-propelled ship generally had to be larger than its conventionally-powered counterparts, since the nuclear power source was heavier than conventional sources when their respective ships were using the same amount of horsepower.[55] This being the case, he used extreme caution and continued to advocate for further research and development on the nuclear reactors intended for surface ships. There was also the fact that if he had more time for research and testing, he would also have more time to explore the cost versus effectiveness of various capabilities.[56]

Overall, McNamara was not hostile towards the prospect of nuclear propulsion. In the 1965 budget, the defense program mentioned longingly an attack submarine fleet that could have half its boats, including six new nuclear attack submarines (SSNs) powered by nuclear reactors by the end of the decade.[57] McNamara announced his conclusion, however, that the *Typhon* frigates were proving too complex, expensive, and large to be a viable capability. Only one of these frigates was intended to have nuclear propulsion, so McNamara's decision is not likely to have been based purely on that issue.[58] The Navy was still concerned with providing fleet defense, and ended up requesting more money for converting another 15 multipurpose ships to *Tartar* DLGs, and for providing five converted destroyers with newer radar systems.[59]

The CVA-67 Carrier — The Push for Reconsideration.

Clearly, nuclear propulsion was not just a question of nuclear carriers. And yet, the debate over whether the next carrier would use nuclear or conventional propulsion has remained more firmly embedded in the historical record.[60] This section will focus specifically on the tug-of-war over the fate of the FY63 carrier (CVA-67) between McNamara on the one hand and the combined efforts of Admiral Rickover, the Navy, and the Atomic Energy Commission (AEC) on the other.

CVA-67 had been authorized as a conventionally-powered aircraft carrier, but Admiral Rickover was determined to revisit the issue to expand the reach of nuclear propulsion.[61] He was optimistic that the AEC and the Navy could address the problem of expense and mass of nuclear power plants with a newly designed four-reactor plant called the A3W. The new plant could fit in the same space as the propulsion system for the CVA-67. In December 1962, Rickover asked the Navy's shipbuilding bureau to examine how to install the A3W plant in the CVA-67. The bureau's ship design division obliged with a determination that the A3W plant would work in the carrier, but would require significant redesign work to accommodate the necessary changes in the propulsion system.[62]

Admiral John "Chick" Hayward, Deputy CNO for Development before taking command of the *Enterprise* carrier group in 1962, was recruited by Navy Secretary Fred Korth to give an operator's backing to nuclear propulsion.[63] Hayward's January 2, 1963, letter conveyed his belief that USS *Enterprise* had performed far better than its conventional counterparts in the operations around Cuba during the missile crisis. He subsequently sent Korth a letter in September, urging nuclear propulsion for the next carrier.[64] His approach was typical of many officers who discounted cost-based arguments in favor of exploiting the latest technologies to ensure future operational victory. Hayward said that a conventional carrier could fight for 3 1/2 days with its onboard provisions of munitions; *Enterprise* could fight for a week, emphasizing his argument by saying, "we should build fighting ships, not floating hotels."[65] In his memoir, however, Hayward admitted numerous problems, including with maintaining the propulsion system and failures of the *Talos*, *Terrier*, and *Tartar* missile systems during President Kennedy's visit and the subsequent cruise to the Mediterranean.[66]

Rickover next sought the backing of the AEC, pointing out that continued development of power reactor technology was a good in itself, as well as having benefits in military operations. Glenn Seaborg, the AEC chairman, wrote to McNamara on January 7, 1963, seeking his support for a four-reactor plant in the carrier. Reportedly, Harold Brown in DDR&E and Charlie Hitch were also supportive of the switch, in addition to most of the Navy.[67] Secretary Korth added his weight to the argument in a January 23 letter to McNamara in which he reviewed the advantages of nuclear propulsion and the need to maintain a program that kept the momentum going for developing the technology.[68]

McNamara was unconvinced that simple technology development was sufficient to justify the expense of converting the CVA-67 to nuclear propulsion. He wanted the Navy to provide more detailed analysis of the role of nuclear propulsion, based on rigorous number-crunching, not vague claims of operational effectiveness. He asked for a study that would examine how nuclear power would affect the carrier task force's composition, defensive tactics, use of supply ships, and number of task forces required. He also wanted to know how the Navy proposed to manage the transition to nuclear power given the natural disruptions a completely new model would have as the force structure changed over time.[69]

The study McNamara wanted would take the Navy past the deadline to bid out the construction of the new carrier. The Bureau of Ships was given the task to proceed with drafting a design for nuclear propulsion, in addition to the oil-fired power plant already in hand. The Navy sent forward to McNamara as much analysis as it could muster by early April, which included Secretary Korth and Chief of Naval Operations Admiral George Anderson's stated belief that all capital ships of 8,000 tons or more should be nuclear-powered, phasing in construction over the next few years.[70]

McNamara rejected the Navy's analysis as insufficient to address his concerns and justify adding more than $600 million to the shipbuilding program over the next 5 years. In an April 20 memorandum, McNamara emphasized a point that would come up repeatedly when debating the merits of various military programs:

> [The] problem is this: Of course nuclear-powered ships
> are better than conventional ships, costs not consid-
> ered. But cost has to be considered because it is a mea-
> sure of what is being given up elsewhere—elsewhere
> in the Navy, the Department of Defense, the Federal
> Government, and the economy as a whole . . . I need to
> know whether nuclear power for surface warships is a
> sensible expenditure as part of any budget, or whether
> your proposal merely makes sense if the implied re-
> ductions in other capabilities are neglected.[71]

The Navy spent the summer months gathering more data and marshalling further arguments in favor of nuclear propulsion. In late September, Korth came back to McNamara with the Navy's concerted opinion that nuclear propulsion provided required advantages in virtually unlimited endurance at high speeds, increased tactical flexibility, the ability to operate in bad weather, or steam around bad weather in ways that a conventional ship would be hard-pressed to do without adequate resupply, the ability to extend the attack across a greater arc, reduced vulnerability stemming from resupply while under threat of attack, and reduced logistical dependence. As for the number of carrier task forces, Secretary Korth asserted that the replacement ratio of nuclear carriers for conventional was five to six, that is, increased combat effectiveness would require one fewer carrier task force for the same result. McNamara was not convinced, but did not close off future nuclear propulsion. He took the Navy analysis to show that the authorized conventional carrier would not reduce effectiveness and directed proceeding with the program as authorized.[72]

McNamara sent Korth a memorandum on October 9 that noted the Navy had yet to complete the analysis he had requested on the advantages of nuclear propulsion, but stated nonetheless:

> On the basis of the analysis available to date, I am not convinced that a net advantage is in prospect. While it is clear that nuclear propulsion would result in some desirable characteristics, the increased cost (particularly in ship construction) remains a serious disadvantage. . . . As a result, I believe the fiscal year 1963 carrier should proceed on the conventionally-powered basis as authorized by Congress. I would like you to take the proper steps to proceed with the construction as soon as possible.[73]

McNamara's decision on the carrier did not end with his October 9, 1963, memorandum to Secretary Korth. Rickover and his compatriots would mobilize the Congressional Joint Committee on Atomic Energy to seek to overturn the decision. The committee's chair, Rhode Island Democrat Senator John Pastore, wrote to McNamara on October 9 to request clarification of the rumors he had heard on the decision to go with a conventional carrier and announced his decision to hold hearings on the topic. Deputy Secretary of Defense Roswell Gilpatric responded to Pastore on October 11 that no decision had been made yet, although internal to the Pentagon, it was clear that McNamara had done just that.[74] Korth had appealed the decision prior to Gilpatric's letter to Pastore, but it was not until October 25, 5 days prior to the announced hearings, that McNamara reiterated his decision and informed Congress.[75]

The Navy and the AEC dominated the hearings on October 30. Secretary Korth testified alongside the new CNO, Admiral David McDonald, Rickover, Vice Admiral Vincent De Poix (the first commander of *Enterprise*), Rear Admiral Hayward, and others. Seaborg represented the AEC, along with several staff members. The lone OSD witness was DDR&E head Brown; McNamara was in Saigon and would testify in mid-November.[76] The committee members were distressed that McNamara had made his decision before the hearings could take place. Even Brown admitted that he had originally supported nuclear propulsion in CVA-67, but also thought more analysis would be needed to back up his inclinations.[77] When McNamara testified 2 weeks later on November 13, he emphasized that Congress had already authorized the carrier as a conventional ship. He was not opposed to nuclear propulsion, but felt Congress had already made its determination the previous year.[78]

The Joint Committee issued its findings early in the New Year, advocating on behalf of nuclear propulsion for CVA-67 and all future first line surface combatants. The committee concluded that "it is an indisputable, demonstrated fact that nuclear propulsion increases the combat effectiveness of our surface warships."[79] McNamara certainly did not dispute this, but the Committee went on to declare that "increased costs attributable to nuclear power are minor."[80] The committee, however, did not have direct jurisdiction over shipbuilding for the Navy, meaning that others would have to carry the banner. Despite a dozen bills in 1964 advocating nuclear propulsion, none passed.[81]

The Two-Reactor Power Plant.

After Kennedy's assassination, several key players in the nuclear navy story changed. Secretary Korth resigned and was replaced by Assistant Secretary of Defense for International Security Affairs Paul Nitze.

Admiral David McDonald had replaced Anderson (who only served one term) as CNO. The AEC continued to lobby McNamara, including hosting him at the Bettis Atomic Laboratory in Mifflin, Pennsylvania, outside of Pittsburgh. McNamara's visit had a result Seaborg, Rickover, and the other commissioners did not intend. He showed great enthusiasm for the work the laboratory was doing on the D1W two-reactor plant. His enthusiasm stemmed from the reduced weight, cost, components, and personnel involved in building and operating the plant, though it would complicate power requirements on a ship where the reactor would provide energy for propulsion and flight-deck operations.[82]

Rickover was not thrilled by the enthusiasm McNamara showed for a two-reactor program, in part because the deadlines to get the FY63 carrier started were passing, as were the decision points for the carriers planned for starts in FY65 and FY67. The next carrier after CVA-67, originally scheduled for FY65, had now slipped its schedule by 2 years. The Navy could have a two-reactor power plant ready for the FY67 ship, but it would be of smaller output than the power-plant under development at Bettis, therefore requiring a smaller carrier similar in size to a World War II-era *Essex* class carrier. A reactor on the scale of the D1W would probably have to wait beyond 1967.[83] The Navy was not interested in such a small ship, which could not carry the number of planes it thought necessary.

Nitze by this point was convinced the Navy would need 15 attack carriers and should fund a nuclear-powered vessel in each fiscal year beginning in 1967 through 1973. He also received assurances that the larger two-reactor power-plant would be ready for a

1967 vessel, if the decision was made quickly and funding assured. Nitze forwarded his recommendations along these lines to McNamara in mid-July.[84] McNamara was still not prepared to approve nuclear power for all carriers, but he agreed that a request to the AEC to proceed with developing a two-reactor power plant would be prudent. He also sent Harold Brown to brief the Joint Committee. According to Rickover and others present, Brown referred to the decision to proceed with conventional power on USS *John F. Kennedy* (as CVA-67 would now be called) by saying, "let's face it, Bob made a mistake."[85] It was not until late August that McNamara, in response to a memorandum from Charlie Hitch, approved nuclear propulsion for the carriers scheduled to begin construction in 1967, 1969, and 1971.[86] But the *Kennedy* would remain a conventionally-powered carrier, largely due to the timing of the decision more than anything else.

McNamara ultimately decided against nuclear propulsion for CVA-67 on cost grounds, claiming that it would cost $440 million compared to $280 million for a conventional carrier. His analysis was not without its flaws. The Congressional Joint Committee on Atomic Energy assailed the assumptions in McNamara's analysis, pointing out that a nuclear carrier could carry 50 percent more aviation fuel and ammunition than a conventional carrier. The Navy's analysis showed that the total life-cycle cost of a nuclear carrier with its air wing over a 25-30 year lifespan is only 3 percent more than a conventional carrier.[87]

McNamara's decision on CVA-67 did not close the debate over nuclear propulsion, nor did McNamara appear to want to do so. On the contrary, he wanted to continue examining the issue and probing how best to accommodate nuclear propulsion in the Navy's surface fleet. From the modern perspective, USS *John F. Kennedy* appears to be a stutter-step along the path to an all-nuclear carrier force.[88] For much of its operational life, *Kennedy* would stand alone as a conventional carrier until its decommissioning in 2007.[89] But at the time, it was similar to other carriers in the fleet. Of nearly 30 carriers at the time (including many of World War II vintage), the nuclear-powered *Enterprise* was in a class by itself.

McNamara Reverses Course — The FY67 Budget.

After winning the fight for a conventionally-powered carrier, McNamara was caught up in a series of efforts to bring Service budgets into line and institute managerial excellence. He also started to push what we would call "Jointness" in weapons development, including trying to force the Air Force and the Navy to work together on a next-generation fighter aircraft, rather than developing two separate aircraft. The TFX program, which eventually became the F-111, was a difficult program that occupied much of McNamara's time.[90]

In the FY1967 budget, McNamara reversed course and requested three nuclear carriers to be built over the next 5 years. He changed his mind in part due to an analysis completed at the Center for Naval Analyses by economist Patrick Parker showing that the costs of a nuclear carrier over its lifetime were less than originally thought. Part of the disparity in cost estimates stemmed from McNamara's systems analysis office assuming that a larger nuclear-powered aircraft carrier would carry an extra squadron of planes, which over the 25 years of operations added $308 million to the cost. This was fully two-thirds of the cost differential between a conventional and nuclear-powered carrier. Since the Navy did not intend to put more planes (at least it stated so at the time) on the carrier, these costs were not accurate.[91] Costs were also reduced by using the new two-reactor cores that were expected to last 13 years, or four times as long as the cores originally installed in *Enterprise*. The Navy had used systems analysis in essence to beat McNamara at his own game. The Navy could now show in reasonable detail and with sufficient sophistication in analysis that the nuclear-powered carrier not only was more effective, but also roughly equal in cost over its lifetime compared to conventional carriers.[92]

Another significant factor weighing on the decisionmaking at this point was the overwhelming enthusiasm for nuclear propulsion developing in Congress. In the words of one participant, "Congress rammed the nuclear fleet down our throat, so I think McNamara just acquiesced in that."[93]

Conclusion.

Analysis played a large role in the decisionmaking over nuclear propulsion, signaling one of the first attempts to use more than military judgment and arbitrary budget ceilings in the process. McNamara did not dispute the operational effectiveness of nuclear propulsion, but insisted on knowing more quantifiably the differences in capability and cost-effectiveness. Nuclear power may have brought an absolute advantage to the tactical and operational employment of the nuclear surface navy, but the relative advantages were what played the larger role in his mind. The Navy wanted to pursue nuclear propulsion to increase endurance, reduce logistics dependency, and provide speed to the fleet. It was not until the mid-1960s that the Navy acquiesced to addressing comparative analyses with concrete data, rather than relying on military judgment to carry the day. The Navy also benefited from powerful congressional allies who saw the need to continue pushing the technological envelope. This constant pressure would eventually wear down McNamara's resistance.

McNamara is often accused of pursuing cost as the driving force behind his program decisions, and to a certain extent he did. But this is not a complete picture. His concern was about relative effectiveness, given a limited budget. The absolute argument did not convince him; the subsequent analysis that demonstrated much smaller cost differences for significantly greater operational effectiveness convinced him to pursue nuclear propulsion. The *Typhon* missile system's development difficulties underlined crucially the dangers of pursuing technology too aggressively and trying to push the deployment of immature and unproven systems. In the end, they would prove much more expensive and damaging to the overall budget than he was willing to bear, for a failure of one system impacted other programs and meant the Navy was unable to fund them.

THE B-1 BOMBER

The next case study examines how changes in requirements and the pursuit of unproven technologies can lead to increasing costs, elongated timelines, and further conflict between civilian leaders and a military service — the Air Force in this case. The B-1 bomber was part of a broader debate over the role of the Service in supporting deterrence and in pursuing a program seemingly to the detriment of other, equally promising technologies. Again, the differing perspectives contributed to the difficulties arising between the Secretary of Defense and the Service. As the critical decision points approached, the assumptions underlying competing sets of analyses became central to the conflict. In contradistinction to the previous case study, the civilian leadership decided to push for newer technologies that showed greater promise, whereas the Air Force seemed more bound to a more traditional platform.

The Air Force of the 1960s was a bomber-centric force. Several Air Force chiefs of staff, including Nathan Twining, Hoyt Vandenburg, and Curtis LeMay, had been bomber pilots. So it is not surprising that a major focus of the Air Force acquisition program in the 1960s was a new manned bomber. This is not to argue that simple ego or institutional bias led the Air Force to focus on buying new bombers. By the time President Carter made his decision to cancel the B-1 bomber in June 1977, numerous studies on replacing the B-52—which was approaching 25 years of service —had been undertaken, and several proposed platforms examined and canceled.[94] Studies had examined the need for a new bomber, and the Air Force had lost repeated battles, such as over the B-70, to find a replacement for the B-52 and the few remaining B-58 bombers in the force.

Establishing the Requirement.

The B-52 production line closed in 1962, but the shoot-down of U-2 pilot Gary Francis Powers in 1960 had the Air Force thinking about the preference for a high-altitude, supersonic bomber supposedly beyond the reach of Soviet air defense missiles. The U-2 incident demonstrated improving Soviet capabilities in this field, and the situation would likely continue to worsen as the Soviets developed newer, more capable, and longer-range missiles.[95] The Air Force pursued a series of studies to examine what the next generation bomber might encompass, yielding an alphabet soup of acronyms. First was the 1961 Subsonic Low Altitude Bomber (SLAB) project, followed by the Extended Range Strategic Aircraft (ERSA) and Low-Altitude Manned Penetrator (LAMP) in 1963. In 1963 the Air Force started two more studies called the Advanced Manned Penetrator (AMP) and the Advanced Manned Penetrating Strategic System (AMPSS). These studies concluded in 1965 and were followed by the Advanced Manned Strategic Aircraft (AMSA) in 1969.[96] The studies tended to support the Air Force's need for a manned bomber, but McNamara, among others, was not convinced of the need for a manned strategic bomber.[97] During this period, the Air Force had begun development of one high-altitude supersonic bomber, the B-70.

False Starts — The B-70 Bomber.

The B-70 program began in 1955 as the Air Force looked beyond the shut down of the B-52 production line to a next-generation bomber. At the same time, missiles under development began to produce intercontinental ranges, meaning that the bomber was no longer the sole means to deliver nuclear weapons on targets in the Soviet Union. The B-70 was originally envisioned as a first-strike platform, but underwent a transformation in the late 1950s and early 1960s into the RS-70, for reconnaissance strike. The idea now was that after missiles delivered a first strike, the RS-70 would follow on, identify those targets that had not been destroyed the first time around, and hit them.[98]

The problem was that McNamara and his systems analysts did not believe the RS-70 would actually function in that capacity. It did not have the computing capacity on board, nor did they believe it could accurately conduct reconnaissance from such high altitudes to determine what targets needed to be hit. They concluded that the Air Force would end up reverting to using it in a bomber capacity—flying at high altitudes to penetrate Soviet air space and drop nuclear bombs on pre-designated targets.[99] In essence, it was no better than a guided missile and provided none of the traditional flexibility of other manned bombers.[100] Given the conclusion that little distinguished it from a missile, it had some drawbacks, such as requiring more time to reach targets than missiles (hours compared to minutes) and was more vulnerable to surprise attack, so it would have to be launched on warning to preclude its destruction on the ground. It also had poor penetrating capabilities: It could deal with enemy interceptor aircraft, but not surface-to-air missile defenses. Finally, the Systems Analysis studies showed that high-altitude flight was the wrong approach to defeating enemy air defenses; low-altitude flight to come in under the radars promised better penetrating capabilities.[101]

Based on this analysis and the projected $11-13 billion cost of fielding three wings of RS-70s, McNamara was unwilling to support more than completing three prototype aircraft. Notably, he estimated that the Air Force had underbudgeted by nearly 50 percent the cost of fielding the three wings that it wanted.[102] He stated in his testimony before Congress in 1963 that the marginal effectiveness of "mop-up" operations conducted by the RS-70 with air-to-surface missiles as opposed to intercontinental ballistic missiles (ICBMs) did not justify the incredible cost.[103] McNamara ultimately canceled the program in 1963, dispatching the Air Force to rethink its bomber requirements.

The Air Force continued to examine its needs throughout the decade, consistently concluding that a next-generation manned bomber was a requirement. The Air Force had two prototype XB-70 bombers that had been built in 1964 with which it conducted flight tests.[104] Meanwhile, McNamara pushed the Navy and the Air Force to build a new tactical aircraft together. The TFX, which later became the F-111, was a program fraught with difficulties, mainly because the Navy's requirements for a carrier-based aircraft conflicted with the Air Force's desire for a heavier aircraft with "dash" speed greater than Mach 1.[105] To accommodate the Air Force's bomber needs, McNamara settled on a "stretch" version of the F-111, the FB-111. From the Air Force's perspective, however, the FB-111 lacked the desirable range and payload for a true strategic bomber.

After President Richard Nixon came to office in 1969, the new Pentagon leadership changed course from McNamara's. SecDef Melvin Laird and his Deputy Secretary David Packard (of Hewlett-Packard fame) encouraged the Air Force to proceed with a new bomber program that would yield an aircraft boasting an unrefueled range of 6,000 miles, top speed of Mach 2.2, flight ceiling of 50,000 feet, and a payload twice that of the B-52.[106]

Difficulties in Executing the B-1 Program.

The B-1 program, like many before and after it, suffered from a number of setbacks during its development. The technology did not fully exist to meet the requirements the Air Force set. Its main objective was to produce a penetrating, supersonic aircraft that could defeat projected Soviet air defense systems. A large component of the debate centered around pushing the plane to higher altitudes to escape the range of surface-to-air missiles, which would require supersonic cruising speeds, or very-low-altitude (less than 500 feet) terrain-hugging flight, in which case sub-sonic speeds are preferable. The B-1 also laid a strong emphasis on using Electronic Counter-Measures (ECM) to defeat Soviet surface-to-air and air-to-air missiles, which required significant technological leaps.[107]

A major concern and focus of congressional oversight during the 1970s was cost growth in DoD programs. The Air Force tracked a dozen programs in the mid-1970s in Selected Acquisition Reports (SARs) to keep abreast of these costs. The programs included airplanes in the Air Force inventory, like the A-10, the F-15, and the airborne warning and control systems (AWACs), as well as missile systems (AIM-7 and AIM-9).[108]

Inflation played a large part in the seeming skyrocketing costs, but even controlled for inflation, costs were increasing. The Air Force anticipated an average of 4.2 percent cost escalation per year from 1977 to 1984 in B-1 procurement costs and nearly 5.8 percent cost escalation per year from 1977 to 1982 in B-1 development costs in base-year FY77 dollars.[109] In August 1975, the Air Force reported to the DoD Comptroller that the estimated development and procurement cost of the B-1 would be $16.974 billion, the largest of the programs captured in the SAR. Only the F-111 ($12.689 billion), the F-15 ($10.743 billion) and the Minuteman III ($9.023 billion) came close.[110] In October, the Air Force reported a further cost increase of more than $500 million to the Comptroller, though this was attributed entirely to "economic change" and not program change.[111]

Congressional Concern.

In addition to cost increases, some members of Congress were concerned the Air Force was not managing the program particularly well and might be obligating funds not authorized or appropriated by Congress. Senator Thomas McIntyre, who chaired the Senate Armed Services Subcommittee on Research and Development, wrote to Secretary of Defense James Schlesinger in January 1975, expressing his concern that several DoD programs had encountered cost increases that took them beyond the funding limits Congress had established for the fiscal year. He was particularly concerned that DoD was allowing contractors to carry these additional costs in anticipation of restitution through FY76 funds — essentially using the following year's funds to make the contractors whole for funds expended in the current year.

Senator McIntyre's concern was real, but also unearthed a significant bind in the way contracts were written. The two parties to the contract agreed on the amounts to be spent in any given year for the contract, but, to prevent the contractor from having to slow or stop work because of unforeseen cost increases, it allowed for the contractor to carry these costs in anticipation of reimbursement later.[112]

The Air Force's contract with Rockwell International included a provision known as the Limitation of Government Obligations (LOGO) clause. The contract noted that the project would be funded on an incremental basis, and the government would not hand over funds to the contractor faster than called for in the contract. The contract then stated, in the usual turgid contract phraseology: "subject to the availability of funds, any costs incurred in excess of the amount allotted hereunder at any time shall, to the extent that such costs are reasonable and allocable, be allowable costs in the event that and to the extent that the Government subsequently increases its allotments hereunder."[113] This would appear to violate the LOGO clause, but the Air Force argued it was in compliance.

The Air Force responded to Senator McIntyre that under the Anti-Deficiency Act, no U.S. Government official is allowed to create an obligation in excess of that authorized and appropriated by Congress. The Air Force then reasoned that the contractor's assumption of carrying costs on behalf of the government does not constitute an obligation on the part of the government, but merely a "conditional" obligation. Although convoluted, the Air Force was essentially saying "yes, but no" to the Senator's accusation. The opt-out for the Air Force is that the reimbursement of the contractor is "subject to the availability of funds," which means that if Congress appropriates no funds, the contractor is left holding the proverbial bag. But the expectation on the contractor's part is that the government, the Air Force in this case, is going to make good in the end and is unlikely to leave the contractor to absorb the costs. The result is negligible in any case, the Air Force then contended. Of a nearly $13 billion total accumulated limit of governmental obligation, the estimated costs were only $15 million more, or approximately 1/10 of 1 percent. Also noted is that the funding level has always been in excess of the bills the contractor submitted for payment, but, because of the timing of work and budgeting at the end of the fiscal year, the occurrence of such cost carrying is temporary and still falls under the LOGO. What this means is that the contractor may be spending monies above the authorized levels, but the contractor was not billing the government for the costs, at least not in the fiscal year in which the costs were incurred.

The Strategic Argument—The FY77 Budget Debate.

The bomber's primary mission during the Cold War was to deliver nuclear weapons to targets in the Soviet Union. The bomber was part of the strategic triad consisting of bombers, ICBMs, and strategic missile-launching submarines. For the first decade or more after the invention of the atomic bomb, warheads were large and bulky enough that bombers provided the most reliable means to deliver them on target. But since the late 1950s, the technology for missiles had developed considerably, and the early 1970s saw the advent of multiple independently targetable reentry vehicles (MIRVs), which allowed one missile to deliver warheads onto distributed targets. This gave rise to a serious examination of whether the bomber force could survive as a viable leg in the strategic triad. The Air Force, and the Pentagon in general, continued to see a future for the bomber in the triad. In his March 1976 congressional testimony, acting Assistant Secretary of Defense for Program Analysis & Evaluation

Pete Aldridge argued that a strategic manned bomber:
- Hedges against ballistic missile failure
- Complicates Soviet attack planning
- Does not represent a disarming first-strike capability
- Provides a visible show of resolve
- Constitutes a flexible, multipurpose system
- Is cost effective[114]

Aldridge's argument left out one other purported advantage of the bomber over a missile — its recall ability. Once a missile is launched, it cannot be recalled; whereas a bomber is subject to recall, therefore giving added time to resolve a crisis. Additionally, a bomber is useful as a means to demonstrate resolve or send a signal, which a missile cannot do. This is what he meant by visible show of resolve. Aldridge addressed the idea of allowing the bomber force to atrophy and pursuing arms limitation talks or more missiles to correct the imbalance with the Soviet Union. He pointed out that the only options available were constrained by the Vladivostok Accord,[115] which set an upper limit on the number of ICBM silos. Therefore, any further missile developments would have to come in the mobile missile field, which the United States, unlike the Soviet Union, had not invested significant resources in. He also noted that allowing the bomber force to phase out would leave the Soviets in the enviable position of having approximately 600 more deployed missiles (2,400 total) than the United States and would not likely agree to future agreements to reduce this advantage.[116] The cost of pursuing a mobile ICBM system would likely match or exceed the $20 billion price tag for a fleet of B-1 bombers.[117]

Aldridge compared the alternatives and asserted that the B-1 provided the most cost-effective means to address the challenges a penetrating bomber would face. He argued that ballistic missiles were not a cost-effective means to suppress or destroy enemy air defenses (though he ignored the crucial question of why you would need to do this if you had already launched a nuclear attack). He also contended that the Joint Strategic Bomber Study the previous year had concluded that cruise missiles would not be able to penetrate air defenses as well as the short-range attack missile (SRAM) or the B-1, though this relied on assumptions about the eventual capabilities of the B-1's electronic countermeasures and the capabilities of the cruise missile which had yet to be built.[118] He went on to address the aging B-52 bomber force, which was approaching 20 years old for the B-52D and 15 years old for the B-52H, the newest of the B-52s. As an aside, he said that "something is going to have to be done, of course, to the B-52 force in order to keep it viable into the 1990's," indicating that the B-1 would be a supplement, not a replacement for the B-52.[119] He concluded that "the most cost-effective bomber force, independent of the total size of the force, has a mix of B-1's with SRAM's for penetration of the high value defended targets and the B-52's which are quite effective carrying cruise missiles for attack of the undefended targets."[120] In his view, then, the B-52 would have to be a penetrating aircraft with short-range nuclear missiles, not the longer-range air-launched cruise missiles some were arguing for.

In response to a letter from Senator Barry Goldwater, Strategic Air Command Chief General Russell Dougherty laid out his strong views on why the B-1 was critical to the future deterrence posture of the United States. Similar to others, he argued that a manned bomber was an essential factor in providing decision-makers flexible options in a crisis. He believed that the manned bomber "offers the United States an overall flexibility of choice and application that is unmatched by an [sic] other weapons system." The bomber could carry large numbers of both conventional and nuclear weapons and deliver to multiple fixed targets with an accuracy over long ranges that he described as "un-equalled."[121] A bomber could also accommodate or be adapted to delivery of many types of weapons, including gravity bombs and standoff launched cruise, ballistic, semi-ballistic, or defensive weapons.

The bomber would fulfill a key role in a cost-imposing strategy on the Soviets, forcing them to continue pouring money into defensive systems (e.g., air defense) instead of offensive systems to address the penetrating bomber threat. He saw the bomber as an economical means to redress the strategic imbalance (i.e., get more nuclear weapons onto launch platforms). He also emphasized the point about bombers as a flexible but visible means to demonstrate resolve. The bomber could wreak havoc on the enemy and do so repeatedly, under certain circumstances. Finally, a bomber can accomplish missions across the spectrum of military options, not just at the strategic end.[122] That said, General Dougherty did not mention that the B-1 was conceived largely as a single-mission aircraft. Its entire design from its supersonic cruising speed to its electronic countermeasures was oriented towards penetrating Soviet airspace and dropping nuclear bombs on fixed targets. His argument underscored the Air Force's belief that a manned bomber was a critical component in the strategic triad. Then he turned to whether the B-1 was the best option for maintaining the bomber force's relevance.

General Dougherty, reflecting the prevailing Air Force view, said that,

> the B-1 [is] the best candidate vehicle reasonably available to satisfy the future requirement for a modern manned penetrating bomber-and to provide the U.S. with the diversified characteristics that are and will be needed in our complementary mix of strategic delivery systems. Not only do I view it as the best, I do not see any other comparable system that can reasonably be expected to do this job as I think it must be done for assurance — or for long-term economics.[123]

He based this assessment on several critical assumptions and conclusions: First, the United States needed manned bombers (and in his letter he included a penetrating bomber as part of the requirement), it needed modern bombers, and the B-1 was the best of the available options. It is unclear whether the last criterion reflected his knowledge of the stealth program (which was not yet a bomber program) or if he meant it to juxtapose with the FB-111, which was the only other modern aircraft besides the B-52 in competition. He emphasized several times that the B-1 was a "real thing," no doubt to dig at B-1's opponents for backing unproven technologies. He said the B-1 was "not a paper study or a theoretical analysis of what *might be* or what *might satisfy* future requirements. The B-1 is here, it is timely, and it is competent — postulated alternatives meet none of those criteria."[124]

General Dougherty's position was guaranteed to carry weight. As Commander-in-Chief, Strategic Air Command, General Dougherty was responsible for the execution of the strategic air attack should the President ever deem it necessary and was the Director of Strategic Target Planning for all strategic nuclear forces.[125] His headquarters at Offutt Air Force Base in Nebraska was the home of the strategic bomber force. His opinion, forcefully expressed, would leave an impression on the assembled Senators. General Dougherty went into the alternatives under consideration and stated that he did not support them because "none of them has stood the tests of long-term sufficiency, cost effectiveness, or supportability over the years ahead. They may have superficial or analytical appeal to some, but they don't measure up with those of us who must maintain and operate our deterrent forces."[126] General Dougherty asserted that the B-52, while carrying the "primary deterrent load" for 20 years, was reaching the limits of its adaptability. He stated that proposed modifications to bring the B-52 forward would be expensive and nonetheless would not remove the need for the B-1. The proposal to build a "stretch" version of the FB-111, on the other hand, would require such upgrades as to render it effectively a new aircraft "with all the expense, time, and testing required" of a new platform. With the Air Force being the primary operators of the FB-111, Dougherty felt that the airplane was too limited in size, range, and payload to constitute an adequate alternative.

Once he dismissed other aircraft, Dougherty moved on to dismiss the air-launched cruise missile (ALCM) as "extremely dangerous, if not ineffective and grossly deficient" as a sole replacement for the bomber. He thought ALCMs could serve a useful secondary role and in low-threat contingencies, but not against a sophisticated air defense system such as the Soviets had. He believed that a stand off platform that launches ALCMs is inherently inflexible, because it cannot penetrate airspace under any circumstances. He would be happy to have the ALCMs *and* the B-1, but not the ALCMs by themselves.[127]

General Dougherty expounded on deterrence theory in general and pointed to the importance of perceptions in its application. He saw the B-1 as representing a "quantum jump" in quality over the existing platforms, which would have visible impact on the Soviets and in demonstrating national will.[128] For him, only deployed forces played into the decision calculus of actors in deterrence; studies, concepts, and operational tests did not—another dig at B-1 opponents advocating for technologies such as the ALCM.[129] And the penetrating bomber "is vital to the assured capability of our deterrent forces. Should we risk delay and then experience any unanticipated challenge to our ICBMs or our SLBMs [submarine-launched ballistic missiles], the imbalance could be ominous, indeed."[130] Here again is the concern about the reliability of the missiles in the arsenal, which at this far remove from the debate seems strange, but at the time was an ongoing concern. The moon landing was barely 8 years removed, and the problems in missile system development were still a concern, whereas bombers seemed a more reliable delivery system after more than 35 years of operational experience.[131]

In response to a question from Senator Barry Goldwater, he admitted that a "selective response" was possible with just the Minuteman or a Poseidon force, but the risks would be greater.[132] SecDef James Schlesinger also raised the issue of ballistic missile reliability in the February 1975 Defense Report to Congress, in which he underlined the role of the bomber as a hedge against failure of the missile systems of the Triad.[133]

General Dougherty estimated that the life-cycle cost of maintaining the B-1 fleet would be 75 percent of that existing B-52/FB-111 fleet.[134] This is in stark contrast to analysis published by the Brookings Institution that year, which was based on best guesses given published and unclassified material. The study's authors, Alton Quanbeck and Archie Wood, believed that the 10-year procurement and operations cost of the B-1 (assuming a 210 plane buy) would be slightly higher than for an equivalent number of B-52s (200, given the larger payload). The B-1s would be slightly more expensive ($71.3 billion in 1976 constant dollars versus $69.6 billion for the B-52s, but operating costs are higher for the B-52s) and the stand off cruise missile carriers indicated costs some $10 billion less.[135]

Air Force Chief of Staff General David C. Jones (who subsequently became Chairman of the Joint Chiefs of Staff in 1978) also advanced a strategic argument for the B-1. His first concern, as with General Dougherty, was the aging fleet of aircraft in the Air Force, both tactical and strategic. He argued that the slide in procurement and accumulated decisions of the previous 10 years meant that the FY77 budget represented a pivotal decision point for the Air Force. He stated "what Congress will decide, influenced heavily by the Committee, is no less than the direction and character of the future Air Force and therefore, in large measure, what strategic policy this nation is to follow."[136] His subsequent strategic argument focused on the relative balance of forces with the Soviet Union.

General Jones ascribed strategic superiority to the period from the end of World War II through the 1960s, when the United States fielded strategic forces superior in number and quality to those of the Soviets. He described it as a "lower risk, but higher cost" option that the United States abandoned for the "modest cost, modest risk" of strategic equivalence, which was the stated policy. He warned against the argument for strategic inferiority in which the balance of forces is irrelevant as long as the United States maintained a minimal capacity to hold a certain percentage of the Soviet population and industrial capacity at risk. This line of reasoning was a setup to lead to an argument that the B-1 was needed to maintain at least strategic equivalence, while a decision to abandon the B-1 would lead to a slide into strategic inferiority.[137] He attacked the Brookings Institution study as dangling the promise of short-term cost savings while arguing for overly narrow mission sets for weapons platforms and leading to the slide into strategic inferiority. He tied the efficiency argument directly back to the strategic argument. His said the B-1 was "our number one priority" in procurement, designed to contribute to equivalence and based on a long list of factors, many of which were similar to Aldridge's and Dougherty's:

- Synergism of the Triad
- Soviet strategic momentum
- Hedge against failures in other systems[138]
- Complicate enemy attack
- Flexible
- Demonstrate resolve
- No first strike implications
- Long useful life
- Large payload/megatonnage
- Highly accurate
- Reusable
- Conventional capability
- Stresses enemy air defenses
- Cost effective.[139]

General Jones was looking to a future where the relative speed of Soviet modernization against American modernization programs that were "standing still" would widen the gap and lead to strategic inferiority (e.g., through Soviet development of the *Backfire* strategic bomber and four new ICBMs). He was worried about heading into the 1980s outfitting the force with the technology of the 1960s and stated that the B-1 was the only program in the near term that could stem the tide of growing Soviet capability and capacity. In his list comparing U.S. and Soviet advantages, the Soviet list was longer, including more delivery systems, more missiles, and more civil defense. His argument clearly showed that he felt the Soviets had the greater numbers and were catching up on quality, while the United States had superior technology for the moment.[140] Finally, General Jones argued that the B-1 program was sitting in the sweet spot of its development timeline: if production was delayed, costs would rise, but enough testing had been done to reduce the risk of untested technologies. He contrasted the B-1 with the C-5 cargo aircraft that had experienced significant problems during development. His analysis of the sweet spot was clearly a judgment, however, for there was no reliable way to project where the program was in its technology maturation and development timeline, and subsequent events would show that significant bugs remained in the program.[141]

The Air Force wanted 244 B-1s, which would replace many, but not all of the B-52s. General Jones estimated that, depending on Strategic Arms Limitations Talks (SALT) limitations, the B-1s would replace less than 50 percent of the B-52s.[142] The Air Force began research and development of the B-1 in 1970 and expected the first operational aircraft to enter the operational force by 1981, with the full 244 buy completed by 1986.[143]

The Brookings Institution versus the Air Force.

It is worthwhile analyzing the Brookings Institution's study on the strategic bomber force, since it served as the basis of much of the political discourse surrounding the B-1 debate in 1976 and 1977, although it played a minor role in the internal decisionmaking for the Jimmy Carter administration.[144] The study was the most detailed unclassified and rigorous analysis of the question surrounding whether to invest in the B-1. It came in the crucial decision year of 1976 and put the Air Force somewhat on the back foot as the Air Force sought to combat the arguments put forth in the study. In fact, the Air Force produced a 32-page critique of Quanbeck and Wood's report, which itself only comprised 116 pages. The Air Force felt it needed to respond to the studies produced by the Brookings Institution because of the influence it supposedly had in Congress and Secretary of the Air Force Thomas C. Reed (who served from January 1976 to April 1977) wanted to be positioned to respond as soon as Quanbeck and Wood's report came out.[145] The Air Force relied on its recently concluded Joint Strategic Bomber Study (JSBS) to rebut Quanbeck and Wood's argument.

Quanbeck and Wood were both former Air Force pilots with significant experience in bombers, so their professional qualifications were significant. Archie Wood went on to serve as Deputy Assistant Secretary of Defense for Strategic Programs under Assistant Secretary of Defense for Systems Analysis Gardiner Tucker from late 1970 to early 1974.[146] Their study examined the role of the bomber in the strategic force and then posited five alternatives for modernizing the bomber leg of the triad. Their five alternatives were:

modified B-52G/Hs with rocket assistance for faster takeoff; B-1s; large transport aircraft such as the C-5 or Boeing 747 modified for strategic use; new aircraft "designed for maximum ability to survive a surprise attack"; and modified large transport aircraft with rocket assistance for faster takeoff.[147] They posited that the bomber force should be designed to attack fixed industrial and urban targets and sized to deliver the equivalent of 400 one-megaton nukes to destroy 75 percent of Soviet industrial capacity. For the bomber force, this would mean 1,200 reliable 200 Kilo-ton nuclear warheads on air-to-surface missiles.[148]

Quanbeck and Wood went on to analyze the existing state of play for the programs under consideration. In 1960 the bomber force was over 1,900 strong with 1,230 tankers to keep them in the air. In 1975 these numbers dropped to 504 and 661, respectively.[149] The B-52G had first deployed in 1959, with an improved range of 10,000 miles, if unrefueled. This was followed by the H model, which extended the range to 12,500 miles, thanks to new turbo-fan engines. At the time of the study's publication, the Air Force was modernizing the B-52G/Hs to carry up to 20 SRAMs (12 under the wings and 8 in bay). Each could also carry four Mark-28 gravity nuclear bombs.[150] The FB-111A could only carry four SRAMs on external pylons and two in the bomb bay, with a shorter range of 4,100 miles.[151] Despite superior performance metrics in all but range, the B-1's real cost growth was 16 percent from 1969 to 1974, yielding a cost of $84 million per aircraft in 1976 dollars, though some defense officials apparently conceded to the study authors that it might cost more than $100 million each.[152] Quanbeck and Wood concluded the high procurement cost of the B-1 would impact the Air Force's ability to modernize the rest of the inventory.[153] In addition, given that the SRAM was the primary B-1 weapon, the costs should take into account restarting the production line, which was closed in 1975. Quanbeck and Wood estimated the costs to be as high as $100 million. They pointed out that ALCMs would have impressive penetration capabilities because of terrain contour matching, allowing flight at 100 feet and very low radar cross section.[154]

They also raised the accusation that the Air Force was slow-rolling the development of ALCMs out of concern that they would be seen as a replacement for the manned penetrating bomber instead of a complement. The ALCM was based on the Navy's cruise missile program. The Air Force had had a program for long-range cruise missiles under the subsonic cruise armed decoy (SCAD) program, which would be a dummy to go in with the B-52s. The Air Force resisted adding a warhead to the SCAD for fear it would be promoted as a stand off weapon.[155] The SCAD program was approved for both uses by the Senate Armed Services Committee in 1972, but the Air Force pursued only the decoy, and the program was canceled in 1973.

The Air Force insisted the cruise missile was a complement to the penetrating bomber, as Brigadier General Harold E. Confer of the Air Staff said in response to questions from Senator McIntyre during the FY75 Military Procurement Authorization hearings:

> it complements the manned bomber, but the bomber will still need to penetrate for the deeper target areas and the harder targets. The missile will complement the bomber in that it will soften the defenses and extend the strike capability. It can be utilized for some of the heavily defended areas' defense suppression to augment the bomber forces coming behind. Therefore, it is still our intent to go ahead and use the penetrat-

ing bomber as it was designed to penetrate the enemy defenses."[156]

Quanbeck and Wood concluded their study by stating "there are marked economic advantages for a bomber force that carries standoff missiles [and] there appear to be no significant military advantages to be gained by deploying a new penetrating bomber such as the B-1 in preference to this alternative."[157]

The Air Force had a distinct advantage in the debate: it could use classified data (which would be more accurate, but also restricted the circle of those able to contest and debate the study's conclusions). The Air Force accused the Brookings scholars of biasing the case against the penetrating bomber before even starting their analysis. The Air Force was challenging the Brookings study's assumptions, including the implicit assumption that enemy air defenses could only be defeated through using large numbers of planes, emphasizing mass over all else.[158] The Air Force argued that their analysis was more sophisticated by taking into account offensive and defensive characteristics such as the command and control structures, geography, radar cross section, weapons effects calculations, and numerous cost-effectiveness reports.[159] For example, they noted that when Quanbeck and Wood estimated the 400-megaton force equivalent in stand off ALCM carriers could destroy 75 percent of Soviet industrial capacity, they were only targeting 50 cities, not the 371 cities that the Air Force believed actually encompassed 75 percent of Soviet industrial capacity.[160] The Air Force said the target set for the force would extend to command and control elements, industry, and military installations.[161] As General Jones stated in his testimony, "the way Brookings saved money was by changing our strategy."[162] He said the Brookings study emphasized a strategy of minimum assured destruction.

In addition, the Air Force faulted Quanbeck and Wood for ignoring force mixes and opting for "pure" comparisons of B-1 forces against B-52 forces and against wide-body ALCM carriers. The JSBS used six equal cost forces (as opposed to Quanbeck and Wood, who used "equal effectiveness" forces), three of which included a mix of stand-off and penetrating aircraft, two of which were penetrating forces, and one of which just looked at the stand-off force.[163] The Air Force also attacked the variables in the model that would produce great sensitivity, such as survivability rates for the bombers on the ground. The Air Force complained that Quanbeck and Wood refused to accept tested crew reaction times, yielding a much starker picture of B-1 survivability than the Air Force believed would be the case. This comes through most starkly in a surprise attack with little warning. Quanbeck and Wood assumed only 31 percent of B-1s would survive if they were not on high alert, while the Air Force estimated more than 95 percent would survive.[164]

The Air Force also noted that the reliance on mass actually denigrated the planned B-1 capabilities, requiring the full force to deliver the weapons required, as opposed to looking at the timing of attack. Relying on supersonic cruise and ECM,

> 17 early arriving B-1s carrying 24 SCAD each could have launched the 400 objects necessary to exhaust the defenses. The remaining aircraft (116 reliable B-1s would be left in the Quanbeck-Wood analysis) each carrying 24 SRAM, could have placed more than twice the number of weapons on target than Quanbeck-Wood assumed to be required.[165]

Finally, the Air Force disputed the cost data of the Brookings study, noting that the study included the cost of a new tanker for the B-1 and far more SRAM and SCAD missiles than the Air Force required.[166] The Air Force argued that once these costs were adjusted and the indirect costs of support (such as bases and nondirect personnel) were subtracted, the B-1 alternative force in the Brookings study would cost approximately the same as the cruise-missile standoff force.[167]

Delaying the Decision.

During the debate over the FY77 Defense budget, B-1 opponents sought to delay a decision on full-up production of the plane until after the forthcoming presidential election. Senator John Culver, a freshman Democrat from Iowa and member of the Senate Armed Services Committee, introduced an amendment to the defense authorization bill in committee in May 1976 to delay the decision until February 1977, but it failed to pass. The aircraft's opponents did not give up, however, and realized that a floor amendment might pass given the right circumstances.[168] The legislative strategy paid off through a combination of clever vote scheduling and waiting until the quorum balance was in their favor. Senator George McGovern, a staunch opponent, introduced an amendment on May 20 that would have deleted all the funds for B-1 production from the bill. This measure predictably failed, but had the benefit of making Senator Culver's amendment seem a benign compromise instead. It passed by a vote of 44 to 37.

The measure was dropped during conference on the bill, but the B-1 opponents now knew they could get the votes and focused on the appropriations bill. In the mean time, the Federation of American Scientists organized a statement from 19 former defense officials that asserted the B-1 was not worth the cost. The signatures included those of Clark Clifford and McGeorge Bundy, which helped pull the rug out from under the argument that the anti-B-1 group was a bunch of "knee-jerk leftists."[169] One name missing from the petition, despite their efforts to recruit him, was former DDR&E head and CalTech President Harold Brown. Senator William Proxmire introduced the amendment into the appropriations bill, successfully this time, so that the decision on proceeding with the B-1 production was no longer Ford's, but would await a new President in 1977—assuming Ford lost to the Democratic contender.[170]

How the Decision Was Made.

The B-1 bomber was unusual in many respects, including the manner in which the decision was made. Given that President Carter had made a pledge during the 1976 presidential campaign to cancel the bomber, the decision was never likely to remain with the DoD. DoD took the decision very seriously, however, and examined numerous studies that compared the relative merits of the B-1's projected capabilities against a set of other platforms, including the B-52 launching an air-launched cruise missile, the FB-111 "stretch," and a cargo plane such as a C-5 or Boeing 747 with ALCMs. The B-1 demonstrated superior performance in a number of scenarios, but the question remained whether the B-1's additional capability justified the expense.[171]

Ultimately, the President would decide, and he relied on an impressive array of data to come to his decision. Secretary Brown provided a sophisticated assessment, but did not strongly advocate any one position.[172] Carter met with Brown on at least four occasions and retired to Camp David to contemplate the large package of information the Pentagon provided.[173] On June 24, 1977, in one of their last meetings before the decision was announced, Brown recommended to the President that the B-1 be canceled.[174] One critical element of the decision package was a Defense Intelligence Agency assessment of future Soviet air defense capabilities. The assessment indicated that the B-1 was likely to provide penetrating capability for between 5 and 10 years longer than the B-52, or into the late 1980s to early 1990s. To some in the White House, this seemed a marginal benefit given the program's cost.[175] The development of ALCMs weighed significantly on the decision. By June 1977, the Air Force had yet to successfully launch an ALCM from an airplane, but development tests were promising.[176] Finally, the B-1 had competition coming in the near future. A highly classified program under the code name Have Blue was advancing the development of new technologies to evade radar detection. While the B-1 relied on ECM to reduce its radar cross section, this new program, which would eventually yield "stealth" technologies, promised to make an airplane virtually invisible by absorbing radar signals. The B-1 would have had a radar cross section of approximately 10 m^2 (compared to 100 m^2 for the B-52 and 7 m^2 for the FB-111A), but a stealth bomber would appear no larger than a bird on radar.[177]

Carter realized the momentum was behind the B-1 and that powerful constituencies in Congress backed the program. The economic difficulties of the 1970s weighed heavily on every decision, and the B-1 would mean jobs in many congressional districts, a fact that many governors and representatives pointed out to Candidate Carter during the election campaign. Carter recognized that deciding whether to move forward was more than a matter of the technical merits of the case, but also overcoming these powerful constituencies.[178]

On June 30, 1977, President Carter held a press conference to announce his decision to cancel the B-1 bomber program. The reaction was as one might have expected: liberals were thrilled, conservatives were aghast, and most members of Congress and the contractors felt blindsided by the decision.[179] Iowa Democratic Senator John Culver called the decision a "victory for common sense—the most constructive and courageous decision on military spending in our time."[180] California Republican Congressman Robert Dornan said, on the other hand, "they're breaking out the vodka and caviar in Moscow."[181] Some in the Air Force and beyond pressed General Jones to oppose the decision more vigorously. He ultimately decided that it was the President's decision, and that "we salute smartly and we will not try to undermine that decision."[182]

Postscript: The Air Force Gets Its Plane.

Jimmy Carter lost the 1980 presidential election to former California Governor Ronald Reagan, who came into office promising economic recovery, fiscal discipline, and a tougher stance on national defense. Although real Defense spending growth began in the last years of the Carter administration, the 1980s are remembered in military circles as the heyday of budget growth under the "Reagan Build-up." Reagan's Secretary of Defense, Casper "Cap" Weinberger, was determined to invest in defense capabilities.[183] Much of the Republican Party felt the Carter administration had dangerously weakened the military and U.S. national security, and the B-1 cancellation was the symbol of that weakness.[184]

Weinberger was not going to be a pushover, however. The Air Force, like all the Services, had a wish list it brought to the new Secretary for approval, but Weinberger wanted to ensure he made the right decisions. At the same time, he felt the Service chiefs and Service secretaries should play a greater role in the budgeting process.[185] Ultimately, the Reagan administration went forward with a 100-plane buy of the B-1, well below the 242 the Air Force had originally sought. President Reagan announced the decision in October 1981 as part of a strategic modernization program to address the persistent and growing Soviet threat.[186] Weinberger stated his belief that the Carter administration was willing to live with too much risk stemming from an aging B-52 bomber force and the uncertain schedule to mature the capabilities of the advanced technology bomber (ATB), which would become the B-2 stealth bomber. He portrayed the investment in the B-1 as a less risky course, with initial operating capability coming in 1986. This would provide a penetrating platform into the 1990s alongside the continued development of cruise missiles.[187] Once the B-2 was fielded, the B-1B would shift from a "strategic penetrator" to a platform for launching ALCMs. The total cost of the 100 B-1Bs would be approximately $258 billion in FY83 dollars once fully fielded.[188]

The B-1B *Lancer* flew its first combat mission in 1998 as part of Operation DESERT FOX, a punitive strike against an array of targets in Saddam Hussein's Iraq.[189] But the B-1 was eclipsed by its bomber cousins, the F-117 and the B-2 *Spirit*, both of which were designed from the start to have conventional and nuclear missions, whereas the B-1's sole mission was as a nuclear penetrator.[190] After less than 20 years in the force and limited use in combat, another Republican administration announced the retirement of a third of the B-1B fleet and consolidation of the remaining planes in 2001.[191]

Conclusion.

The B-1 bomber was an ambitious program in terms of technology (e.g., electronic countermeasures and escape module) and scale. The Air Force started from a decision that the B-52 was aging, and a replacement was needed. This narrow focus on the bomber allowed many of its opponents to grab the initiative in the strategic debate over the role of the penetrating bomber in a broader strategy of deterrence and response. It was unquestionably an expensive program, but the Air Force felt that the expense was worthwhile to keep up with the Soviets as they developed more sophisticated air-defense systems. The civilian Defense leaders needed to address a broader question, given promising new technologies that could render the race between penetrating bombers and air defense systems obsolete. Much as HMS *Dreadnought* led to an apparent wholesale obsolescence of entire classes of ships in the early 20th century, stealth technology and cruise missiles offered the possibility of a technological leap over the air defense problem. The Air Force started with the assumption that a manned, penetrating bomber was still an integral part of the strategic force, whereas some of the civilian leadership and external experts sought to challenge that view.

Congress played a strong role on both ends of the argument. The extended timelines for developing the prototypes and making procurement decisions gave the bomber's congressional opponents time to muster their arguments against the program. The proponents of the program built a loyal caucus of B-1 devotees, many of whom had flown in a prototype and dealt directly with Rockwell executives. Rockwell, for its part, sought to influence not just Congress, but public opinion on the bomber by sponsoring surveys and public outreach to establish the B-1 as crucial to national defense.

THE CRUSADER ARTILLERY SYSTEM

You're going to lose this one.[192]

— Army Officer

It was a victory, I guess.[193]

— Senior Defense Official

The debate over the Army's Crusader artillery system is indicative of how heated and vicious the conflict between Defense's civilian leadership and a military service can get. As with the B-1, the Crusader program tried to push the technological envelope, ultimately to the program's detriment. The opposing sides had vastly different perspectives on the program that grew wider apart as the debate progressed. Eventually it would devolve into accusations of deceit and mutual recriminations. The program began as an examination of how to address certain tactical problems, but eventually grew to signify, in some observers' views, everything that was wrong with the Army at the dawn of the 21st century. Crusader proponents and opponents put forward absolute arguments, but ultimately the civilian leadership in Defense made its decision based on a relative comparison between Crusader and other technologies, balanced against the strategic direction they laid out for the Armed Forces.

Origins of the Debate.

Texas Governor George W. Bush came to The Citadel, a state-sponsored military academy in South Carolina, in the fall of 1999 to give a speech establishing his national security credentials. Except for part-time service in the Texas Air National Guard and as the head of the Texas Guard, Governor Bush had no experience in international and security affairs. His time as governor had focused on domestic issues such as education, and he needed to establish his vision for the military and national security. The Citadel would provide a friendly atmosphere to lay out his ideas.

Much of Bush's speech focused on contrasting his approach to the military and overseas operations from that of the incumbent President, Bill Clinton. He said, "[S]ending our military on vague, aimless, and endless deployments is the swift solvent of morale."[194] But he also emphasized the need to take advantage of the:

> opportunity . . . created by a revolution in the technology of war. Power is increasingly defined, not by mass or size, but by mobility and swiftness. Influence is measured in information, safety is gained in stealth, and force is projected on the long arc of precision-

guided weapons. This revolution perfectly matches the strengths of our country—the skill of our people and the superiority of our technology. The best way to keep the peace is to redefine war on our terms. Yet today our military is still organized more for Cold War threats than for the challenges of a new century—for industrial age operations, rather than for information age battles. There is almost no relationship between our budget priorities and a strategic vision. The last 7 years have been wasted in inertia and idle talk. Now we must shape the future with new concepts, new strategies, new resolve. . . . As president, I will begin an immediate, comprehensive review of our military—the structure of its forces, the state of its strategy, the priorities of its procurement—conducted by a leadership team under the Secretary of Defense. I will give the Secretary a broad mandate—to challenge the status quo and envision a new architecture of American defense for decades to come. We will modernize some existing weapons and equipment, necessary for current tasks. But our relative peace allows us to do this selectively. The real goal is to move beyond marginal improvements—to replace existing programs with new technologies and strategies. To use this window of opportunity to skip a generation of technology. This will require spending more—and spending more wisely. We know that power, in the future, will be projected in different ways.[195]

He went on to describe a future force that was lighter, faster, and more lethal than before, able to deploy rapidly and require little logistical support. He even spoke of mobile long-range artillery. It was an ambitious vision, but it left a number of questions open. What does it mean to "skip a generation" of technology? How do we balance lethality, speed, and force protection? Interestingly, many people involved in the Crusader case later on recalled then-Governor

Bush speaking directly about Cold War-era weapons systems "like the Crusader and V-22," but these lines do not appear in the text of his speech.[196] In fact, he came into some criticism from the likes of *The Washington Post* for his lack of specificity.[197] His chief aides on national security at the time, Condoleezza Rice, Richard Armitage, and Dick Cheney, all refused to comment on specific platforms or program decisions in the immediate aftermath of the speech. Armitage may have obliquely referred to Crusader when he said programs or planned upgrades may be deferred or canceled if the platforms "are difficult to deploy."[198] As the presidential campaign entered the election year, then-Governor Bush mentioned the Crusader as one example of wasteful spending, stating, "it looks like it's too heavy. It's not lethal enough."[199]

Army Transformation.

Less than a month after Governor Bush spoke at the Citadel, General Eric Shinseki, the new Chief of Staff of the Army, addressed one of the most powerful organizations affiliated with the Army—the Association of the U.S. Army (AUSA). On October 12, 1999, Shinseki delivered the keynote speech at AUSA's annual meeting and outlined his vision for Army transformation. In many respects, his vision seemed to accord with Governor Bush's. He wanted a faster, lighter, more lethal Army.

Shinseki began by noting that:

> our superb heavy divisions remain unequalled in their ability to gain and hold ground in the most intense, horrifying direct fire battles we could imagine. And with our investments in strategic mobility, they become the decisive element in the major theater wars

we envision. But these same divisions are challenged to get to other contingencies where we have not laid the deployment groundwork as well. And once deployed, it takes significant cost to sustain them. Our magnificent light forces — the toughest light infantry in the world — can strike lightning fast but lack staying power, lethality, and tactical mobility once inserted.[200]

Shinseki wanted to leverage greater reachback communications and intelligence to reduce deployed support elements, so that if it is not deployed "some maneuver commander won't have to feed it, fuel it, move it, house it, or protect it." He advocated C-17 deployable systems that could also fit a "C-130-like profile" for intra-theater tactical movement. He said that the Army would "prioritize solutions which optimize smaller, lighter, more lethal, yet more reliable, fuel efficient, and more survivable options." Shinseki was asking for a lot. He laid down a marker for combat-capable brigades that could deploy in 96 hours anywhere in the world, followed by a full division in 120 hours and five divisions in 30 days.[201]

In an article published in the AUSA "Green Book," Shinseki described a "nonnegotiable contract with the American people to be a *warfighting Army-persuasive in peace, invincible in war-preeminent in any conflict.*" To achieve this pre-eminence, Shinseki defined six objectives: (1) increasing strategic responsiveness; (2) developing a long-term strategy to improve jointness; (3) developing leaders for joint warfighting and for change; (4) integrating the active and reserve components; (5) fully manning warfighting units; and (6) providing for the well-being of Army personnel, civilians, and families.[202]

The origins of the Crusader artillery system long predate Shinseki's tenure as Chief of Staff. The primary self-propelled artillery platform for more than 40 years had been the M109 artillery system, the then-current version being the M109A6 Paladin.[203] In the mid-1980s the Army launched an effort to modernize the heavy forces, with the Paladin replacement part of the effort. The heavy force modernization effort, which combined three heavy-tracked and armored vehicles into one program, proved unwieldy as a single program and unraveled in 1991. The artillery platform survived the collapse of the Soviet Union and proceeded towards Milestone B (system development and demonstration) as a standalone program in 1992.[204] The program had ambitious technology development goals, including using liquid propellant, a mid-barrel cooling system, an auto-loading system, higher rates of fire, and improved accuracy.[205] In the aftermath of the Soviet Union's collapse, the Army refined the requirements of the system, lowering the desired range from 50 kilometers unassisted range to 40 kilometers of rocket-assisted range. The rate of fire was reduced from 14 rounds per minute to 10, and the weight was reduced to increase mobility. The Army held firm on the accuracy required.[206]

The system was to deploy in the mid-1990s, but ran into significant problems, particularly in maturing the technology for the liquid propellant. Artillery has used roughly the same technology for over 100 years for propelling the munition, which is based on solid propellant pre-measured into bags. Once the gunner has determined how far he has to fire, he can plot a firing solution that tells him how much solid propellant to use. During the American Civil War, this was measured out by hand, but through the years a system of bags with equal amounts of propellant emerged, which required adjusting the number of bags depending on how much propellant was needed. Five bags might go in the chamber, and the other three would be discarded later. The attraction of liquid propellant was the ability to precisely meter out the amount of propellant desired.

The problems were formidable, however. One problem came from the simple physics of injecting a liquid into a tube filled with air. The liquid would fill the tube, but an angled gun will have a small pocket of air at the top, which results in uneven burn. Additionally, the liquid was dense and could not be carried in an ordinary tanker truck; the rocking back and forth of the fluid could unbalance the truck or break through a normal thin-skinned tanker. So the Army moved to 55-gallon drums to hold the corrosive propellant. Eventually the Army had to abandon liquid propellant after a series of spectacular failures.[207]

By 1994, the Crusader had emerged as its own program under the name with which it would gain its fame. In 1998, the Army asked RAND to "explore the utility of the Crusader system to the future of the Army."[208] The RAND study looked at the ability of Paladin to support the maneuver forces, which the Assistant Vice Chief of Staff of the Army felt was limited due to limited mobility and a slow rate of fire.[209] The report looked at the ability of the M109 in comparison to the Bradley fighting vehicle and the Abrams tank. It found that the M109 had shortcomings in terms of firepower (both rate of fire and range), cross-country mobility, manual loading, and survivability from counterfire.[210]

The M109A6 Paladin was fielded in 1993 with improved fire control and the ability to navigate better than its predecessor, the M109A5. It could receive fire missions via radio and had computer-calculated firing data, but the Crusader would yield better results than this.[211] The report concluded that the Crusader, which at this point would weigh 55 tons, or 110 tons with its resupply vehicle, was a near-term solution to partner with the Bradley and Abrams, but would not mesh with the vehicles foreseen for the Army After Next, which at the time the Army planned to field starting in 2015.[212] Revealingly, the report advocated the Crusader as a technology demonstration and maturation vehicle for technologies planned for the Army After Next.[213]

For much of the Army, the report underlined the principal problem with the Paladin: it was not as capable as other systems available on the world market. The Paladin had a shorter maximum range than the German PzH 2000, Chinese PLZ45, Russian 2S19, and British AS90, among others. Additionally, it carried less on-board ammunition, and had a lower rate of maximum fire. The Paladin could compete with most platforms in weight (it was lighter than all except for the Slovak ZTS, a wheeled system), on-road speed, and crew size (most had a crew of four or five).[214] The Crusader, as planned in 1998, would improve on all these parameters.

Changes to the Program, 1999-2001.

By the time Shinseki took over the Army (he had been Vice Chief of Staff of the Army), the Crusader had been in the works for more than 10 years and still not emerged as a prototype or fielded platform. After Shinseki's AUSA speech, the Crusader was the subject of several conversations at the highest levels of the Army, not as a candidate for cancellation, but to see how the Crusader could be saved.[215] The Crusader played into the Army's vision of itself as the ultimate

68

master of maneuver warfare, involving massive firepower to overwhelm the enemy along a broad front. There is no indication that Shinseki contemplated cancelling Crusader (despite its apparent incongruent place in his vision for a more agile force), but he did want to bring its weight down to make it more deployable. Some have argued that Shinseki protected the Crusader as part of a grand bargain to gain support within the Army for his transformation vision.[216]

The Crusader was meeting some of its targets. In January 2000, the prototype gun SPH1 fired 60 rounds at an average of 9.78 rounds per minute. The Milestone II criteria only called for six rounds per minute, so the Crusader prototype had already come close to meeting its final objective of 10 rounds per minute, and it loaded the entire cycle of 60 rounds through the auto-loader in just 6.5 minutes.[217] Having completed this round of testing, the prototype was shipped to Yuma Proving Grounds in Arizona for a scheduled 2 1/2 years of live fire testing. Despite this success, the Army's FY2001 budget submission was projected to scale back the Crusader purchase, in part to invest funds in transforming towards the Shinseki vision of a lighter, more mobile, and lethal force.[218] The funding would provide $1 billion to stand up the initial Brigade Combat Teams and invest in the Future Combat Systems science and technology development programs, which anticipated at the time, according to then-Secretary of the Army Louis Caldera, fielding the Objective Force around 2012.[219] A key piece of the budget was reducing the Crusader buy from 1,138 to 480 guns (and an equal number of resupply vehicles). Over the course of FY2000 to FY2014, this yielded, according to Caldera, $11.2 billion in reduced expenditures the Army wanted to put towards its transformation.[220] The Army still wanted the Crusader, but was running into problems funding its full list of desired equipment. Caldera conceded that the Crusader was mainly important to the heavy forces "that are going to be with us for another quarter-century."[221]

Implementing the Transformation Agenda.

Donald Rumsfeld had served as Secretary of Defense once before, at the end of the Ford administration, but the Pentagon he inherited in 2001 seemed in many respects not to have changed much in the ensuing 24 years. Like McNamara before him, Rumsfeld had a mandate for change from the President and the determination to establish control over the Department to steer it in new directions and shake it out of its perceived lethargy.[222] During his confirmation hearing, he said:

> we need to ensure that we will be able to develop and deploy and operate and support a highly effective force capable of deterring and defending against new threats. This will require a refashioning of deterrence and defense capabilities. The old deterrence of the cold-war era is imperfect for dissuading the threats of the new century and for maintaining stability in our new national security environment.[223]

Rumsfeld was limited in his ability to address acquisition issues because of his complex personal finances that he sought to hold on to. As with other people who enter high-level government service, he was advised to divest himself from his investments.[224] During his first year in office, he recused himself from decisions on acquisitions in an attempt to avoid this divestment.[225] He wanted to run the Pentagon his second time around using the benefits of more than 2 decades in the private sector, including a successful stint as the chief executive officer (CEO) of the pharmaceutical company G. D. Searle. His concept was to use a corporate board structure. He would provide the vision and rely on senior staff to implement that vision. The Service secretaries—Tom White of the Army, Jim Roche of the Air Force, and Gordon England of the Navy—would be his senior vice presidents in charge of the Pentagon's "business units."[226] All three had come from the private sector and understood the need for cost-cutting and decisive action. Rumsfeld expected the same approach to translate to the DoD.

In mid-April 2001, Rumsfeld met with his three service secretaries and told them that they would have to look at programs to cut in order to fund transformation in the DoD. This meeting was his attempt to give marching orders to his "corporate board." The F-22 fighter, Crusader, and the Comanche helicopter may not have been explicitly discussed but were clearly in mind, given how much press they had received during the campaign and afterwards. Any time media outlets discussed potential transformation, these platforms were first to be mentioned as candidates for cancellation.[227]

Rumsfeld convened a series of review panels to undertake a fundamental review of the DoD strategy and programs in the spring of 2001. The panels included his senior advisors and some outside experts, but the deliberations were largely opaque to outside observers and even many Pentagon civil servants and military officers.[228] In April 2001, one of the panels recommended cancelling the Crusader, citing a perceived disjuncture between the program's capabilities and the new defense strategy that relied on swift power projection and joint fires. One official said, "the

71

Crusader effectively got the ax from the panel because it didn't fit the agenda. It's a wonderful system—for a legacy world."[229] But this was the recommendation of just one panel, and Rumsfeld was under no obligation to accept the recommendations.

At least 10 other panels convened at the same time had yet to report their findings, leading some in the Services to hold back on engaging too aggressively.[230] Some members of Congress, such as Oklahoma Representative and former college football star J. C. Watt, were less reticent. He termed the panel's recommendation "unwise" and released a statement emphasizing that "no final decisions have been made."[231] Deputy Secretary of Defense Paul Wolfowitz felt that the panel had overstated the case against the Crusader. He believed the early arguments against the Crusader did not offer adequate alternatives.[232]

Crusader was always a target for elimination, though not always at the highest levels. In early May 2001, Comptroller Dov Zakheim reviewed with senior defense officials a series of slides that Secretary Rumsfeld was due to take to President Bush. The briefing provided some strategy, but also posed some potential program decisions for the FY2002 budget, including retiring all the B-1 bombers, stretching out the V-22 procurement, and cancelling the Crusader.[233] The White House and senior Defense officials decided not to proceed with these proposed changes, but it was likely that further discussions would occur.

The Impact of 9/11 on the Department's Strategy.

On September 10, 2001, Secretary Rumsfeld delivered a speech to an audience of civilian DoD employees arguing that the bureaucracy was a "threat" and an "adversary." He promised to liberate the Department from itself.[234] Additionally, work on the *Quadrennial Defense Review* (QDR) was wrapping up after a long and brutal summer of fights, internal reviews, and backtracking on plans for radical changes to force structure. And then the terrorist attacks of September 11, 2001 (9/11) seemed to render much of the discussions moot. The United States was at war and needed to mobilize. A significant outcome of the events of that day was that thoughts about reducing the active duty Army by two divisions were quickly shelved.[235]

Canceling a program is not the only way to transform, but it is a powerful signal. The revised FY2002 budget request sought more money, but did not cancel programs. The budget request for fiscal year 2003 working inside the Pentagon had to be revised in light of 9/11 and the war in Afghanistan. But some programs were still under consideration for termination, revision, or retention, particularly the F-22, the V-22 tilt-rotor aircraft, the DD(X) destroyer, the Crusader, and the Army's Future Combat Systems—all big-ticket projects that had had troubled histories of one sort or the other.

Despite preliminary talk about cutting programs, the President's budget request submitted in February 2002 still contained $475.6 million for continued development of the Crusader artillery system. At this point, Deputy Secretary Wolfowitz had heard from many constituents that the Crusader should be cancelled, that it was a Cold War relic and was completely inappropriate for the current or future security environment, but Wolfowitz felt that the Army had made enough of an argument to continue developing the system. In his mind, the critics' claims seemed overblown and offered few or no alternatives.[236] Rumsfeld argued that cancelling programs was not an ideal measure of transformation, but his critics dismissed such arguments as "lame" and accused him of surrendering to the Services and pronounced his transformation efforts dead on arrival.[237]

Secretary of the Army Thomas White and General Shinseki testified before Congress in March on the program, among many others, and on the Army budget. Hawaii Senator Daniel Inouye, who was the Defense Appropriations Subcommitee Chairman, gave White and Shinseki the opportunity to defend the Crusader, noting that "almost every day there's some article in the paper" criticizing the program. White responded by recalling the days when he grew up in an Army outgunned by the Soviets and other adversaries. He said the United States had not fielded a new artillery cannon on a "brand new" chassis since the early 1960s and that the M109 was on its sixth major modification.[238] Though this was technically true, it was somewhat disingenuous, given that the M109A6 variant was less than 10 years old at this point.

Shinseki added his belief that accusations terming Crusader a Cold War relic were primarily based on the excessive weight of the system, but since it had gone on a "slim fast diet" (as Secretary White termed it), it would be down to 40 tons. He asked whether the Army wanted a system even lighter than that. Answering his own question, he said that naturally a lighter weapon would be desirable, but the existing technology and requirements for stability, while ensuring long-range heavy artillery, simply ruled out anything lighter. Shinseki said, "you just can't overcome the mechanics."[239] Despite his call for platforms that were C-17 deployable to theater and tactically deployable by C-130, he emphasized that the Crusader was destined to go into the heavy counterattack corps, 3rd Corps, which would deploy by ship. To paint the picture of how much additional fire power fewer Crusaders could provide, he said that "four Crusaders in Kosovo would have put steel in every inch of that province, and that's the capability we've needed for years."[240]

As late as April 9, 2002, Deputy Secretary Wolfowitz was still defending the Crusader in public, though not as unequivocally as the Army was. At a Senate Armed Services Committee hearing, Michigan Senator and Committee Chairman Carl Levin asked Wolfowitz about the Crusader, noting its weight, inability to transport on the C-130, and shorter range than other Army fire systems. Wolfowitz responded that "the Crusader of today is not the Crusader that people were talking about some 2 years ago. The Army . . . responded to the appropriate criticism that it was much too heavy to move anywhere by redesigning the vehicle and reducing it so that the weight of the total system is down by about a third."[241] He noted that there were future planned systems and also precision artillery munitions—the Excalibur round—in development or on the drawing board. Senator Levin pressed Wolfowitz for an assessment of Crusader, to which he responded that "my summary is that Crusader is . . . a little bit in between. It is a system that brings us some dramatic new capabilities, but if we can bring forward some of the transformational capabilities more rapidly, we might see ways to put that Crusader technology into a different system."[242] It was hardly a ringing endorsement and gave some indication of where he was leaning at this point.

Privately, however, Wolfowitz had his doubts. His doubts grew over the course of several months and a series of meetings with the Army and OSD staff to review the analysis. Further, Wolfowitz felt that the Army was not giving him the straight story. Several of his advisors brought to his attention that the Army seemed to be slipping the timelines for development of the precision-guided artillery munition known as Excalibur just days after Wolfowitz had asked about speeding up its deployment.[243]

Programs, Analysis, and Evaluation (PA&E) head Barry Watts sent Wolfowitz a memo on April 24 containing the analytical background for canceling the Crusader. His memo was strongly worded and clearly advocated canceling the system, using a broader picture to elevate the discussion above a debate over the merits of different artillery systems. It pointed to the entire "fires" picture, including systems organic to the Army, as well as Air Force and Navy assets. He stated that "this short paper . . . provides enough information and analysis for you and the Secretary to reach a decision on Crusader." Watts wanted to avoid a situation in which the Army could drag out the decisionmaking process, aided and abetted by OSD Policy, including another round of studies on the Crusader in the *Defense Planning Guidance*.[244] The memo went through Wolfowitz's front office the next day. On Friday, April 26, 2002, Wolfowitz met with his senior OSD advisors, including acquisition chief Pete Aldridge; Aldridge's deputy, Mike Wynne; Rumsfeld's special assistant, Larry DiRita; Barry Watts; and Wolfowitz's special assistant, Jaymie Durnan. The meeting covered a number of funding issues before coming around to a discussion of the Crusader.

Wolfowitz emphasized his desire to use all the funds in the current budget (the FY02 budget had $475 million) and the next year's budget ($485 million) for precision weapons, Future Combat Systems Research and Development (R&D) and global positioning system (GPS) guidance to retro-fit 155-mm artillery rounds. His point was to ensure that the Army still benefited from the funds and the decision to cancel the Crusader could not be "unraveled."[245] This was an OSD-only meeting, however, and Wolfowitz had yet to discuss his thinking with the Army.

Ten Days of Decision.

On April 29, 2002, Deputy Secretary Wolfowitz and Aldridge went to see Secretary Rumsfeld to tell him their decision to cancel the Crusader. Rumsfeld asked if they had done all the analysis to support the decision. When they responded in the affirmative, Rumsfeld okayed the decision and told Wolfowitz to carry out the necessary next steps. Upon returning to his office, Wolfowitz summoned Army Secretary Tom White to inform him of the decision.[246] Secretary White asked for more time to think about the implications of the decision. Wolfowitz had told him the Crusader was to be cancelled, and that he, White, should examine the impact of this decision on the Army programs, particularly investing in other programs such as the future non-line of sight cannon and "net-fires." Wolfowitz wanted to find out how to spend the money within the Army program to move these other programs forward.[247]

It is unclear whether Secretary White understood this was the decision. Several participants in the meeting and close to the situation had conflicting assessments of the focus of the meeting. Ray DuBois felt that the Deputy Secretary had not clearly conveyed his decision to White. He felt that Tom White came away from the meeting thinking he had managed to get a reprieve of 30 days before a final decision would be made.[248] According to Jaymie Durnan, Wolfowitz went back to Rumsfeld after the meeting with White to tell him that he had given White 30 days to study the problem. Rumsfeld took this to mean the Crusader had not, in fact, been cancelled.[249] In Washington, and especially the Pentagon, a decision is often not taken as final, but as an invitation to further debate.

The next day (Tuesday, April 30), Wolfowitz apparently decided that another 30 days would yield nothing new that countless other reviews and analyses had not already revealed. He discussed the decision with Rumsfeld, who agreed. Wolfowitz then met with Secretary White later that afternoon to reiterate his decision. Secretary White allegedly complained that the Secretary and Deputy Secretary did not know what they were doing.[250] Shortly after the meeting, a set of Army talking points strongly advocating the Crusader system and accusing the Secretary of Defense of trying to score transformation points while endangering soldiers' lives began to appear on fax machines on the Hill and in the Pentagon.[251] The Army talking points set off a fire storm, with one participant telling Secretary Rumsfeld that it constituted rank insubordination on the Army's part.[252]

The cat was out of the bag, but the formal steps still remained. Secretary Rumsfeld notified the White House of the decision on May 7 and the next day held a press conference to publicly announce the decision. After some brief remarks, he turned the press conference over to Wolfowitz and White to explain the decision.

The decision to cancel the program caused consternation on the Hill. Some members of Congress were apoplectic, asserting that the decision had come out of the blue and, more crucially, had not included consultations with them.[253] Oklahoma Senator James Inhofe asserted that Chairman of the Joint Chiefs Richard Myers, Vice Chairman Peter Pace, General Shinseki, Army Vice Jack Keane, several combatant commanders, and Generals Schwartz and LaPorte from U.S. Forces Korea had all told him they were not apprised of the decision prior to the May 8 public announcement.[254] The Senate Armed Services Committee wanted to get to the bottom of the issue and convened a hearing on May 16, 2002.

The first session featured Rumsfeld, Wolfowitz, Aldridge, and Wynne; the second session featured General Shinseki. Senator Levin convened the hearing, stating that the two fundamental questions the Committee wished to have answers to were "what changed in the Department's view of the Crusader program, particularly in the last several weeks . . . [and] are the advantages and capabilities of Crusader sufficient to justify the costs?"[255] Secretary Rumsfeld said the decision to cancel Crusader resulted from months of review and balanced risk across the four areas identified in the 2001 QDR, not just based on near-term warfighter needs.[256] He stated further that "tough choices are made at the margins, often between programs that are both desirable, and both wanted, but nonetheless, choices have to be made . . ."[257] He pointed to the success in Afghanistan that demonstrated that flexibility, speed of deployment and employment, the problems of restricted access to the area of operations, and the integration of ground forces with air assets all pointed to options other than the Crusader.[258]

Shinseki's testimony emphasized his belief that the Army still needed the Crusader, again noting its superior range, speed, and volume of fire. He noted that cancellation was an option in the Army's 30-day study, but he had not had the opportunity to examine the OSD analysis supporting cancellation.[259] He also said that "if you have imprecise locations, or if you just know that there's enemy forces out there, but you don't have them accurately located, precision doesn't help you very much," essentially shooting holes in one of the primary OSD arguments for other platforms.[260] Most of OSD's arguments, and particularly Rumsfeld's focus, were on precision. The Army still wanted mass.

Essence of a Decision: The Tactical versus the Strategic.

The Army is a tactical organization; even Army officers will acknowledge this.[261] The Army's focus on the Crusader came down to a concern about how the artillery functioned tactically on the battlefield, whether it could keep up with other armor forces, and if it could outgun the adversary. The senior civilian leadership in the Department had other concerns: how can we shape and pay for a new military that will carry out the missions of the 21st century?

The Crusader suffered from its extended development timeline. As one Army officer involved with the program said, "it just took too long to get it to the field."[262] The repeated delays in fielding the Crusader and changing requirements, particularly in 1999 and 2000, meant that the Crusader would be fielded in 2008, which at the time was forecasted as the year when the Future Combat System would be fielded. This begged the obvious question: Why would the Army continue to pursue a weapons system like Crusader when its replacement was due to take the field at the same time?[263] Second, most Army analysis compared artillery systems to artillery systems, but ignored other fire systems, such as the multiple-launch rocket system (MLRS), High Mobility Artillery Rocket System (HIMARS), and attack helicopters. At one point during the analysis, PA&E realized the oversight and added these other systems to the picture.[264]

But this only explains how the civilian leadership decided that the Crusader had to be canceled. What brought the decision about at the time it happened? This is a subject of some conjecture, because it is unclear when the real transition occurred. Many in the Army believed at the time and still believe that the decision was purely political and not based on analysis.[265] Part of the answer lies in a growing sense in OSD that the Army was not presenting an honest case for the program. The changes in the Excalibur program, including a slipping timeline and a change to make it exclusively a Crusader munition, gave senior DoD officials an uneasy feeling. Additionally, some independent-minded Army officers pointed out to Wolfowitz that the need for speed to keep up with the Abrams tanks and Bradley fighting vehicles was a red herring: the entire Army could not keep up with the armor vehicles, let alone the artillery. Finally, the White House was exerting pressure on the Pentagon to show results in the effort to transform the Army. The 2003 budget request with Crusader funding had raised numerous questions and requests for additional justification from White House officials, including the Vice President, even after the budget submission in February.[266]

Summary.

One senior OSD official summarized the Crusader decisionmaking process by saying "we made just about every mistake in the book. We didn't understand the process . . . we had no guidance on if you want to take this on, here's what you need to do . . ."[267] The arguments on both sides can seem compelling — the Army had longstanding concerns about the ability to provide fire support to forces against superior forces or peer-competitors, whereas the civilians in OSD had trouble understanding how the Crusader fit into a strategic framework of future warfare based more on precision than on mass. The arguments against Crusader were long-standing. By 2002, it had become a poster child for what many thought was wrong with the Army. Some believed that Rumsfeld and others saw it as a prime example of the Army unable to adapt to future warfare.[268] The lack of a coherent case and the impression that the Army was changing its story eventually swayed the civilian leadership against the Crusader.[269]

CONCLUSION AND OBSERVATIONS

In an April 1963 address to the American Society of Newspaper Editors, McNamara said that "the Secretary of Defense — and I am talking about any Secretary of Defense — must make certain kinds of decisions, not because he presumes his judgment to be superior to his advisers, military or civilian, but because his position is the best place from which to make these decisions."[270] Under Title 10, the Service secretaries and chiefs have the responsibility to equip the forces, but the SecDef has the responsibility to look across the Defense enterprise and ensure the requirements of the Department as a whole are met. The case studies examined demonstrate that the interests of a Service can conflict with those of the Department.[271]

There are asymmetries of information in acquisition. The Services often have larger staffs dedicated to generating requirements, evaluating alternatives, and overseeing programs. Despite that, the Secretary of Defense must have sufficient capacity to take an independent look at major weapons programs from a strategic and, yes, budgetary perspective. As Donald Rumsfeld said at the May 16, 2002, hearing on the Crusader, often the question is not whether a particular program is a good program or not (though there are some that fall in this category), but whether it makes sense from a relative cost and comparative capabilities perspective. This provides the kernel of conflict.

The DoD today relies to a great extent on the systems and procedures originally put in place under McNamara, though subsequent SecDefs have made their own modifications. The system was designed to provide the information a Secretary would need to make informed decisions and trade-offs. But trade-offs often require picking winners and losers, which is made more difficult when lives are potentially on the line. Systems analysis provides one means to make these difficult choices and isolate the emotional from the rational.

Operational commanders in particular show disdain for the systems analysis approach. Chick Hayward (the commander of the *Enterprise* task force during the Cuban Missile Crisis and somewhat of a maverick in his own right) typifies this attitude:

Another, even more weird exercise [McNamara] and his "Whiz Kids" were running constantly was what he called "cost-effective analysis," studies on what a proposed new weapon system would do compared to an existing one it was to replace, to reveal if that would be worth the increased (usually) item cost. In effect, he was using arithmetic to make judgment calls on military combat capability, and usually poor ones, at that, because his statistics ignored half the real-world equation, the "people" factor. Yet, in spite of "Management" McNamara, we in "labor" knew that how well a ship or aircraft performs depends not on what the engineering specs say it can do but on how well it's maintained, how skilled the pilot or skipper is, and how committed, even heroic, he is in combat. Synergism between man and machine is what wins battles, not "cost-effectiveness."[272]

Such sentiments continue to this day, as evidenced by the reaction of some within the Army to Rumsfeld and Wolfowitz's impending decision to cancel the Crusader. The notorious talking points sent to the Hill from the Army's Office of Legislative Liaison accused Rumsfeld of scoring cheap political points at the expense of soldiers' lives.

The preceding case studies demonstrate that certain elements are constant in the ongoing civil-military debate over "how much is enough" and what is the most effective way to meet national security and defense needs. Future civilian and military leaders would do well to heed a few lessons from these cases.

Lesson 1. Perspective is everything. The Services will invariably seek to maximize tactical and operational effectiveness. The Secretary of Defense must look holistically at the strategy and match that against his concerns about the budgetary constraints. The Services must also deal with budgetary constraints, but can often look to other Services as sources for "fudging" the Service top-line. This is the approach the Air Force, in particular, took in its very early days as an independent Service after World War II.

Lesson 2. Although absolute arguments tend to dominate debate, they rarely provide the insight and sophistication required to make an informed decision. Services will—as many others do—make arguments about the absolute necessity of a weapons program, without which future conflict will leave the United States the loser. Air Force officers routinely cite April 1953 as the last time an American soldier was killed by enemy fixed-wing air attack, pointing to the need for enduring air dominance (not just superiority). Naval officers often cite the aircraft carrier as more than four acres of floating sovereignty, while ignoring its growing vulnerability to ballistic and cruise missile technology. These emotive, absolutist arguments have the benefit of forcefulness and presenting a clear choice. They are also largely useless in the modern debate over capabilities. Dynamic, relative arguments are more accurate in providing a supposition against which to challenge the desires of one or the other party. It is not enough to say one program is absolutely "good" or "bad," but to compare it to other systems, and more importantly, to fix it in a larger strategic argument.

Lesson 3. The iron triangle lives, and Congress plays a strong role. Decisions cannot be made without actively engaging the power brokers on the Hill. Because many DoD decisions result from compromise or forceful personalities trying to push through their decisions, the senior leadership is often left trying to convince a skeptical Congress of an imperfect case. Additionally, the senior leadership has fought so many battles already, that sheer exhaustion and the press of thousands of other decisions further sap energy from the crucial fight on the Hill. The Secretary of Defense can win individual battles through force of will (such as happened in the Crusader case), but rarely maintain a sustained campaign. His efforts are complicated by the strong liaison presence the military Services keep on the Hill. The Secretary of Defense's legislative assistants have a tough time counteracting this influence. Finally, congressional members vociferously protect their right to ask military officers their professional opinions on any military issue and often give more weight and respect to those opinions than they give to the Department's civilian leadership.

Lesson 4. Cost will always play a critical role. Although public political discourse often emphasizes our willingness as a country to provide the Soldier, Sailor, Airman, and Marine the equipment he or she needs to fight and win, tough choices are made all the time, and cost will carry a great deal of weight in any discussion. Military officers may be uncomfortable with debates that center on cost-effectiveness, but they cannot avoid it.

Lesson 5. Assumptions are critical and should be rigorously tested and questioned. Parties to a debate over military requirements often do not recognize the basic critical assumptions that support their understanding of the situation. Failure to recognize these differences and bring them out for debate means more time spent in unresolved debate.

Lesson 6. Developing technologies often take longer to mature than originally anticipated and may exceed the cost and schedule originally allotted. The pursuit of the better often comes at the expense of the good, and in the case of the Crusader may have resulted in its cancellation. If the Army had pursued a less ambitious platform, arguably it would have its new artillery piece today.

Understanding these lessons is only the start, however. Civilians and military officers should vigorously debate military requirements. The differences in perspectives are essential to democracy and contribute to better results in the end. That having been said, understanding the basis for each other's point of view can immeasurably help smooth this process, to the benefit of all. So what is the Secretary of Defense to do? The lessons identified above highlight that there are no easy answers. The six lessons are dilemmas that every Secretary of Defense faces and will continue to face. The key is to explicitly understand these lessons from the outset and develop decisionmaking strategies that take them into account constantly.

Secretary of Defense Robert Gates has attempted to provide the Services with full voice in decisions on major weapons programs, while limiting the unending debates and rearguard actions to save programs. He asked Service chiefs to sign nondisclosure agreements to get a better handle on the narrative DoD would present to Congress on the FY2010 budget.[273] As part of such agreements, the Secretary should set limits on debate. Too often, a new Service chief will appeal for more time to analyze an issue even though his Service has had sufficient time as an enterprise to analyze and debate an issue. This recommendation is not intended to stifle or shackle Service chiefs from doing their job and defending their service's prerogatives; rather it is to set reasonable limits on debate in an environment where a decision is often taken as an invitation for more strenuous debate.

Decisionmaking bodies proliferate in the Pentagon: we have seen the advent of Deputy's Advisory Working Group (DAWG), Senior Level Review Group (SLRGs), Senior Level Review Councils (SLRCs), Joint Requirements Oversight Council (JROC), and other bodies with representatives from the military and civilian sides of the DoD. Some have suggested using one of these bodies, such as the DAWG to vigorously debate a program's merits — perhaps with CAPE (Cost Assessment and Program Evaluation) playing the "prosecutor" and the Service as the "defendant" — to expose the relative merits of a program and then hold secret balloting amongst the participants. The Deputy Secretary would then take the results of those debates forward to the Secretary for his final decision.[274] Some form of this idea is worth considering, but will require a method to look more broadly than single programs, which can look indispensible when examined in isolation.

Debates in these higher counsels should give more relative weight to the combatant commanders, particularly the Joint Forces Command (which is responsible for developing doctrine and concepts for how the Joint Force will fight in the future). The combatant commanders are the ones who have to "fight the force" and are more naturally inclined to think jointly about the employment of forces than their Service chief counterparts. Although the combatant commander has a near-term focus on what it would take to fight now and for the duration of his term, this counterbalances the Service chief's focus on long-term acquisition. The role of Service secretaries needs to be addressed as well. President Bush and Secretary Rumsfeld sought to implement a "corporate board" approach, but soon found their Service secretaries beholden to their Services, rather than serving as brakes on the Services' appetites. More often, a Service secretary is chosen for his knowledge of the Service, meaning that he is much more likely to be an advocate than an ax-man. This trend appears to be continuing under the current administration.[275] The Secretary of Defense needs Service secretaries who can find a happy medium between advocate and ax-man; someone who will ask the tough questions and bring a healthy dose of skepticism, while seeking to understand the Service's needs and address them innovatively.

At the same time, the Secretary of Defense will continue to need civilian staff of varied talents across the enterprise. Systems analysis as embodied in PA&E is a useful tool, but only one of many. OSD Policy and the Office of the Under Secretary of Defense for Acquisition, Technology, and Logistics (AT&L) must also provide their perspectives and continue to recruit talent from across the experience and educational spectrum. Finally, the power brokers in Congress must be a part of the deliberative process and not an afterthought. Well-thought-out policies in the national interest will inevitably run into members who will say, as Senator Chris Dodd said following the announced closeout of the F-22 buy, "we've beaten [Secretary Gates] in the past and we'll beat them [sic] again."[276]

The DoD has seen record budgets in recent years, but the era of war supplementals will soon end.[277] As the budget declines or experiences near-zero real growth in future years, the balancing act between recapitalization of the force and pursuing new programs will come into sharper relief, increasing the likelihood of increased debate between the Department's civilian leadership and the military over how best to invest in future capabilities. The Secretary of Defense has the

unenviable task of balancing these competing requirements and implementing a strategy that will have significant consequences for how the Services develop in
the future.

REFERENCES

Interviews.

Ambassador David Aaron, former Deputy National Security Advisor

Honorable Claude Bolton, former Assistant Secretary of the Army (Acquisition, Logistics and Technology)

Dr. Harold Brown, former Director of Defense Research and Engineering and Secretary of Defense

Mark Cancian, former Director, Land Forces Division, Program Analysis & Evaluation

Ray DuBois, former Under Secretary of the Army and former Deputy Under Secretary of Defense (Installations & Environment)

Jaymie Durnan, former Special Assistant to the Secretary and Deputy Secretary of Defense

Lieutenant Colonel (Ret.) Jan Jedrych, former staff member, Headquarters Department of the Army, Logistics Directorate

Dr. Christopher Lamb, former Deputy Assistant Secretary of Defense (Resources and Plans)

Tom Mullins, Deputy Assistant Secretary of the Army

Colonel John Scott Turner, former project manager, Crusader artillery system

Dr. Victor Utgoff, former National Security Council staff member

Dr. Barry Watts, former Director, Program Analysis & Evaluation

Honorable Thomas White, former Secretary of the Army

Dr. Paul D. Wolfowitz, former Deputy Secretary of Defense

Honorable Michael Wynne, former Principal Deputy Under Secretary of Defense (Acquisition, Technology & Logistics)

Archival Material.

National Archives II, College Park, Maryland

Record Group 200, McNamara Papers

Record Group 330, Office of the Secretary of Defense

Record Group 340, Secretary of the Air Force and Chief of Staff of the Air Force

Record Group 341, Headquarters U.S. Air Force

Record Group 428, Department of the Navy

Published Sources.

Adams, Gordon. *The B-1 Bomber: An Analysis of Its Strategic Utility, Cost, Constituency, and Economic Impact.* New York: Council on Economic Priorities, 1976.

Borosage, Robert. "Rumsfeld's Surrender." *The Washington Post*, February 7, 2002, p. A25.

Bruner, Edward F. and Steve Bowman. "Crusader XM2001 Self-Propelled Howitzer: Background and Issues for Congress" RS21218. Washington, DC: Congressional Research Service, Updated June 25, 2002.

Burns, Robert. "Army Secretary Holds Out Possibility of Criminal Prosecutions." *The Associated Press*, February 2, 2000.

"Carter's Big Decision: Down Goes the B-1, Here Comes the Cruise." *Time*, July 11, 1977, available from *www.time.com/time/printout/0,8816,919040,00.html*.

Carter, Jimmy. *Keeping Faith: Memoirs of a President.* New York: Bantam Books, 1982.

Carter, Luther J. "Nuclear Carriers: Studies Convince the Skeptics." *Science*, Vol. 151, No. 3716, March 18, 1966, pp. 1368-1371.

Cohen, Eliot. *Supreme Command: Soldiers, Statesmen, and Leadership in Wartime.* New York: Free Press, New York, 2002.

Coulam, Robert F. *Illusions of Choice: The F-111 and the Problem of Weapons Acquisition Reform.* Princeton, NJ: Princeton University Press, 1977.

Drew, Christopher. "Obama Wins Crucial Round in Senate Vote on F-22." *New York Times,* July 22, 2009, p. B1.

Duncan, Francis. *Rickover and the Nuclear Navy: The Discipline of Technology.* Annapolis, MD: Naval Institute Press, 1990.

Enthoven, Alain C. and K. Wayne Smith. *How Much Is Enough? Shaping the Defense Program 1961-1969*, Santa Monica, CA: RAND Corporation, 1971, 2005.

Feaver, Peter D. and Richard H. Kohn, eds. *Soldiers and Civilians: The Civil-Military Gap and American National Security.* Cambridge, MA: MIT Press, 2001.

"Gov. Bush and Defense." *The Washington Post*, Editorial, September 26, 1999, p. B06.

Hayward, John and Carl Borklund. *Bluejacket Admiral: The Navy Career of Chick Hayward.* Annapolis, MD: Naval Institute Press, 2000.

Holder, William G. *The B-1 Bomber.* Blue Ridge Summit, PA: Aero, 1988.

Hood III, Ronald Chalmers. "Bitter Victory: French Military Effectiveness during the Second World War." In Allan Millett and Williamson Murray, eds. *Military Effectiveness: The Second World War.* Boston, MA: Unwin Hyman, 1990.

Hoopes, Townsend and Douglas Brinkley. *Driven Patriot: The Life and Times of James Forrestal.* New York: Vintage Books, 1993.

Huntington, Samuel. *The Soldier and the State: The Theory and Politics of Civil-Military Relations.* Cambridge, MA: Belknap Press, 1957.

Janowitz, Morris. *The Professional Soldier.* New York: Free Press, 1960, rev. 1971.

Jenkins, Dennis R. *B-1 Lancer: The Most Complicated Warplane Ever Developed.* New York: McGraw Hill, 1999.

Kaplan, Lawrence S. *et al. History of the Office of the Secretary of Defense: Volume V: The McNamara Ascendancy 1961-1965.* Washington, DC: Office of the Secretary of Defense, 2006.

McMaster, H. R. *Dereliction of Duty: Lyndon Johnson, Robert McNamara, the Joint Chiefs of Staff, and the Lies that Led to Vietnam.* New York: HarperCollins, 1997.

McNamara, Robert S. *Statement before the House Armed Services Committee on the Fiscal Year 1965-69 Defense Program and 1965 Defense Budget*. Washington, DC: U.S. Government Printing Office, January 27, 1964.

_____. *Testimony of the Secretary of Defense as Inserted in the Congressional Record*, April 11, 1963. 88th Cong., 1st Sess., pp. 6424-6425.

Matsumura, John M. *et al. Assessment of Crusader: The Army's Next Self-Propelled Howitzer and Resupply Vehicle*. Santa Monica, CA: RAND Corporation, 1998.

May, Ernest. *Strange Victory: Hitler's Conquest of France*. New York: Hill and Wang, 2000.

Myers, Steven Lee. "Bush Candidate for Defense Job Sees Overhaul." *The New York Times*, January 12, 2001, p. A1.

Nuclear Propulsion for Naval Surface Vessels: Hearings Before the Joint Committee on Atomic Energy. Washington, DC: U.S. Government Printing Office: 1964, 88th Cong., 1st Sess., Hearings from October 30-31 and November 13, 1963.

Quanbeck, Alton H., and Archie L. Wood. *Modernizing the Strategic Bomber Force: Why and How*. Washington, DC: Brookings Institution, 1976.

Roherty, James M. *Decisions of Robert S. McNamara: A Study of the Role of the Secretary of Defense*. Coral Gables, FL: University of Miami Press, 1970.

Scarborough, Rowan. "Bush proposes military changes; Futuristic weapons, land forces on list." *The Washington Times*, September 24, 1999, p. A1.

_____. "Pentagon Staff to be Trimmed by 15 percent; Bureaucracy an adversary, Rumsfeld says." *The Washington Times*, September 11, 2001, p. A1.

Shanker, Thom, and James Dao. "Defense Secretary Wants Cuts in Weapons Systems to Pay for New Technologies." *The New York Times*, April 16, 2002, p. A25.

Shinseki, Eric K. "Beginning the Next 100 Years." *Army*, Vol. 49, No. 10, October 1999, pp. 21-28.

von Clausewitz, Carl. *On War*. Howard, Michael, and Peter Paret, eds. Princeton, NJ: Princeton University Press, 1976.

Wade, Nicholas. "Death of the B-1: The Events Behind Carter's Decision." *Science*, Vol. 197, No. 4303, August 5, 1977, pp. 536-539.

Weinberger, Caspar W. *Fighting for Peace: Seven Critical Years in the Pentagon*. New York: Warner Books, 1990.

_____. *Department of Defense Annual Report to the Congress for Fiscal Year 1983*. Washington, DC: U.S. Government Printing Office, February 8, 1982.

Wood Archie L. "Modernizing the Strategic Bomber Force Without Really Trying-A Case Against the B-1." *International Security*, Vol. 1, No. 2, Autumn 1976.

ENDNOTES

1. Samuel Huntington, *The Soldier and the State: The Theory and Politics of Civil-Military Relations*, Cambridge MA: Belknap Press, 1957, serves as the basis for the ensuing discussion. Other works include Morris Janowitz, *The Professional Soldier*, New York: Free Press, 1960, Rev. 1971; and more recently Eliot Cohen, *Supreme Command: Soldiers, Statesmen, and Leadership in Wartime*, New York: Free Press, 2002; and H. R. McMaster, *Dereliction of Duty: Lyndon Johnson, Robert McNamara, the Joint Chiefs of Staff, and the Lies that Led to Vietnam*, New York: HarperCollins, 1997.

2. See, in particular, his chapter on the military profession, Huntington, *The Soldier and the State*, pp. 7-18.

3. Quoted in *Ibid.*, p. 11.

4. Carl von Clausewitz, *On War*, Michael Howard and Peter Paret, eds., Princeton, NJ: Princeton University Press, 1976, p. 102.

5. The largest empirical study of civil-military relations in recent years was led by scholars of the Triangle Institute for Security Studies, which discussed military experience for members of Congress and the attitudes of civilian elites towards defense spending in aggregate, but did not address the gap in military experience and its impact on decisionmaking internal to the Department of Defense. See Peter D. Feaver and Richard H. Kohn, eds., *Soldiers and Civilians: The Civil-Military Gap and American National Security*. Cambridge, MA: MIT Press, 2001.

6. Ernest May, *Strange Victory: Hitler's Conquest of France*, New York: Hill and Wang, 2000; and Ronald Chalmers Hood III, "Bitter Victory: French Military Effectiveness During the Second World War" in Allan Millett and Williamson Murray, eds., *Military Effectiveness: The Second World War*, Boston, MA: Unwin Hyman, 1990, pp. 221-255.

7. Robin Cross, *Citadel: The Battle of Kursk*, London: Michael O'Mara Books Ltd, 1993, p. 70.

8. Indeed, Secretary of Defense Donald Rumsfeld at times sounds as though he is channeling Robert McNamara in his 2002

testimony about the Crusader artillery system. See pp. 61-82 for more details.

9. David Halberstam, *The Best and the Brightest*, New York: Random House, 1969, pp. 227-229.

10. Townsend Hoopes and Douglas Brinkley, *Driven Patriot: The Life and Times of James Forrestal*, New York: Vintage Books, 1993, pp. 320-325, 328-331, 339-340, 351-364, and 405-410.

11. Alain C. Enthoven and K. Wayne Smith, *How Much Is Enough? Shaping the Defense Program 1961-1969*, Santa Monica, CA: RAND Corporation, 1971, 2005, p. 11.

12. *Ibid.*

13. *Ibid.*, p. 34.

14. *Ibid.*, pp. 35, 38.

15. *Ibid.*, p. 48.

16. *Ibid.*, p. 56.

17. *Ibid.*, p. 64.

18. *Ibid.*, p. 78.

19. *Ibid.*

20. *Ibid.*, p. 1.

21. National Archives II, Record Group (RG) 200, McNamara Papers, Box 10, FY62 Budget—Draft Message to the President. Kennedy apparently never fully read this memorandum and indicated that future memos were not needed in such depth (the draft memo ran to over 100 pages), but McNamara continued to use the draft memorandum to the President as a tool to steer the Department's programs.

22. *Ibid.*

23. Notably, *Enterprise* is still in the active fleet and has more than recouped its initial procurement cost in terms of fuel savings.

24. Author interview with Dr. Harold Brown, February 2, 2009.

25. Francis Duncan, *Rickover and the Nuclear Navy: The Discipline of Technology*, Annapolis, MD: Naval Institute Press, 1990, p. 99.

26. *Ibid.*, p. 101.

27. *Ibid.*, p. 103.

28. James M. Roherty, *Decisions of Robert S. McNamara: A Study of the Role of the Secretary of Defense*, Coral Gables, FL: University of Miami Press, 1970, p. 141.

29. Duncan, p. 101.

30. NAII, RG200, 130:75/3/04, McNamara Papers, Box 25, "Nuclear Powered Surface Ships," memorandum dated February 7, 1962.

31. Secretary Harold Brown noted that subsequent study showed the difference in deployment times to areas of operation ended up being measurable in hours, not days, which somewhat diminished the alleged advantage of nuclear power. Author interview with Dr. Harold Brown, February 2, 2009.

32. NAII, RG200, 130:75/3/04, McNamara Papers, Box 25.

33. *Ibid.*

34. Lawrence S. Kaplan *et al.*, *History of the Office of the Secretary of Defense: Volume V: The McNamara Ascendancy 1961-1965*, Washington DC: Office of the Secretary of Defense, 2006, pp. 72-95.

35. Quoted in *Ibid.*, pp. 72-73.

36. *Ibid.*, p. 77.

37. *Ibid.*, p. 78.

38. *Ibid.*, p. 80.

39. *Ibid.*, p. 81.

40. NAII, RG200, 130:75/3/04, McNamara Papers, Box 20, "FY64 Program Decisions," dated July 13, 1962.

41. NAII, RG200, 130:75/3/04, McNamara Papers, Box 21, "FY64 Budget, Secretary of Defense Statement before the Senate Armed Services Committee," dated January 21, 1963.

42. *Ibid.*

43. NAII, RG200, 130:75/3/04, McNamara Papers, Box 25, Draft Memorandum for the President, "Navy Shipbuilding Program and Ship Force Structure, excluding the Polaris Program, FY1964-1968," dated October 31, 1962.

44. *Ibid.*

45. Robert S. McNamara, *Statement before the House Armed Services Committee on the Fiscal Year 1965-69 Defense Program and 1965 Defense Budget*, Washington, DC: U.S. Government Printing Office (GPO), January 27, 1964, p. 70.

46. NAII, RG200, 130:75/3/04, McNamara Papers, Box 25, Navy Department Memorandum to the Secretary of Defense, "Shipbuilding and Conversion Program," dated November 9, 1962.

47. NAII, RG200, 130:75/3/04, McNamara Papers, Box 25, Undated memorandum, "Nuclear Powered Surface Ships, FY1964 Issues."

48. The *Typhon* combat system was planned for use on frigates, destroyers, and cruisers, hence, the reference to the *Typhon* for different classes of ships. It would be canceled in 1963.

49. NAII, RG200, 130:75/3/04, McNamara Papers, Box 25, Charles J. Hitch Memorandum to the Secretary of Defense, "Possible Adjustments to the Secretary of Defense Recommended Shipbuilding Program," dated November 9, 1962.

50. *Ibid.*

51. *Ibid.*

52. NAII, RG200, 130:75/3/04, McNamara Papers, Box 25, Navy Department Memorandum to the Secretary of Defense, "Shipbuilding and Conversion Program," dated November 9, 1962.

53. NAII, RG200, 130:75/3/04, McNamara Papers, Box 20, "FY63 and FY64 Program Changes, Navy Surface Fleet."

54. Duncan, p. 135.

55. NAII, RG200, 130:75/3/04, McNamara Papers, Box 25, Memorandum on "Nuclear Powered Surface Ships," dated February 7, 1962.

56. Robert S. McNamara, *Statement before the House Armed Services Committee on the Fiscal Year 1965-69 Defense Program and 1965 Defense Budget*, Washington, DC: GPO, January 27, 1964, pp. 69-70.

57. *Ibid.*, p. 74.

58. *Ibid.*, p. 76.

59. *Ibid.*

60. Most books about the period focus on the debate over the CVA-67, which would later be called USS *John F. Kennedy*, than on the other components of the fleet. See Roherty for one example.

61. Francis Duncan, *Rickover and the Nuclear Navy: The Discipline of Technology*, Annapolis, MD: Naval Institute Press, 1990, p. 129.

62. Duncan, p. 130.

63. Hayward, a vice admiral at the time, turned down Kennedy's offer of a fourth star and the position of Deputy CIA Director in favor of demotion to two stars and command of the carrier

division. John Hayward and Carl Borklund, *Bluejacket Admiral: The Navy Career of Chick Hayward*, Annapolis, MD: Naval Institute Press, 2000, p. 264.

64. *Ibid.*, p. 280; Duncan, p. 130.

65. Hayward and Borklund, p. 258.

66. *Ibid.*, p. 266.

67. Duncan, pp. 131-132.

68. *Ibid.*, p. 132.

69. *Ibid.*, p. 133.

70. *Ibid.*, pp. 134-135.

71. Quoted in *Ibid.*, p. 135.

72. *Ibid.*, p. 136.

73. *Nuclear Propulsion for Naval Surface Vessels: Hearings Before the Joint Committee on Atomic Energy*, 88th Cong., First Sess., Hearings from October 30-31 and November 13, 1963, Washington, DC: GPO, 1964, p. 244.

74. Duncan, p. 137.

75. *Nuclear Propulsion for Naval Surface Vessels*, p. 25; and Duncan, p. 138.

76. Admiral Hayward remembers McNamara being present at the hearing and names October 26th as the date of testimony. This is unlikely, given that the 26th was a Saturday and Congress held no business that day. Hayward and Borklund, pp. 280-281. Paul Nitze was also present, but made no substantive comments. He was Assistant Secretary of Defense for International Security Affairs at the time and would not be appointed Secretary of the Navy until the end of November.

77. *Nuclear Propulsion for Naval Surface Vessels*, p. 41; and Duncan, p. 138. Dr. Brown's testimony focused on the uncertainty of the advantages to be accrued from a nuclear-powered surface fleet and sought to balance those uncertainties against the projected costs. Despite the uncertainty, he provoked some laughter when he claimed that: "I come to the problem with a prejudice in favor of nuclear ships" even though his testimony was taken to mean he was against them. In fact, the tenor of his testimony was not to come down strongly on one side or the other, but merely to point out the complex analytical questions involved.

78. Duncan, p. 139.

79. *Nuclear Propulsion for Naval Surface Vessel*, p. iii.

80. *Ibid.*, p. iv.

81. Duncan, p. 140.

82. *Ibid.*, p. 141.

83. *Ibid.*, p. 142.

84. *Ibid.*, p. 143.

85. *Ibid.*, p. 143.

86. *Ibid.*, p. 146.

87. Luther J. Carter, "Nuclear Carriers: Studies Convince the Skeptics," *Science*, Vol. 151, No. 3716, March 18, 1966, p. 1370.

88. The ship was tentatively named *United States*, but was redesignated *John F. Kennedy* following President Kennedy's assassination.

89. Available from *www.nvr.navy.mil/nvrships/details/CV67.htm*.

90. For an in-depth look at the TFX, see Robert F. Coulam, *Illusions of Choice: The F-111 and the Problem of Weapons Acquisition Reform*, Princeton NJ: Princeton University Press, 1977.

91. Carter, p. 1370.

92. *Ibid.*, p. 1371.

93. Author interview with Harold Brown, February 2, 2009.

94. Of note at the time of this writing (2009), the B-52 is still in the inventory and will likely remain until 2040 at least, more than 75 years from its advent.

95. William G. Holder, *The B-1 Bomber*, Blue Ridge Summit, PA: Aero, 1988, pp. 1-2.

96. *Ibid.*, p. 2.

97. Dennis R. Jenkins, *B-1 Lancer: The Most Complicated Warplane Ever Developed*, New York: McGraw Hill, 1999, p. 23.

98. NAII RG200 130: 75/3/04 McNamara Papers, Box 25, Draft Memorandum for the President on the FY1964 Budget, December 3, 1962.

99. *Ibid.*

100. Enthoven, p. 244.

101. *Ibid.*, p. 245.

102. NAII, RG200, 130: 75/3/04, McNamara Papers.

103. *Testimony of the Secretary of Defense as Inserted in the Congressional Record* April 11, 1963, 88th Cong., Sess. 1, pp. 6424-6425.

104. Holder, p.5.

105. Robert F. Coulam, *Illusions of Choice: The F-111 and the Problem of Weapons Acquisition Reform*, Princeton, NJ: Princeton University Press, 1977, pp. 71-73.

106. Gordon Adams, *The B-1 Bomber: An Analysis of Its Strategic Utility, Cost, Constituency, and Economic Impact*, New York: Council on Economic Priorities, 1976, p. 1.

107. Author interview with Dr. Harold Brown, February 2, 2009.

108. NAII, RG340, 170: 56/20/03, SAFFM Chron File, Folder 2023-75, Air Force Selected Acquisition Reports for 1975. It is unclear from the SAR what the real origin of the cost growth is—for the B-1 it notes that "revised spare estimates" were involved, but lists the major component stemming from "Economic Change," which is attributed to revised Assistant Secretary of Defense (Comptroller) (ASD[C]) guidance of February 18. The economic change reflects a $33.4 million growth in B-1 and a $2M "program change" for a net change in the program funding of $31.4M. The F-15 had $128.7 million deducted under "economic change" which represented most of the net $185.4M decrement to the 12 programs.

109. NAII, RG340, 170: 56/20/03, SAFFM Chron File, Box 1 of 10, Assistant Secretary of the Air Force (Financial Management) Memorandum to Assistant Secretary of Defense (Comptroller) on Out-Year Escalation in December 31, 1974, Selected Acquisition Reports, dated February 14, 1975.

110. NAII, RG340, 170: 56/20/03, SAFFM Chron File, Acting Assistant Secretary of the Air Force (Financial Management) Arnold Bueter Memorandum to the Assistant Secretary of Defense (Comptroller), dated August 5, 1975. Although dated early August, the data reflect costs from June 30.

111. NAII, RG340, 170: 56/20/03, SAFFM Chron File, Proposed Memorandum from Assistant Secretary of the Air Force (Financial Management) to the Assistant Secretary of Defense (Comptroller) on Selected Acquisition Reports, dated October 23, 1975.

112. NAII, RG340, 170: 56/20/03, SAFFM Chron File, Assistant Secretary of the Air Force (Financial Management) Memorandum to Assistant Secretary of Defense (Comptroller) on Senator Thomas J. McIntyre's Letter of January 6, 1975, dated February 11, 1975.

113. *Ibid.*

114. Edward C. Aldridge, Acting Assistant Secretary of Defense for Program Analysis and Evaluation, testimony before the Senate Armed Services Committee on the FY77 Authorization for Military Procurement, March 10, 1976, p. 2892.

115. The Vladivostok Accord is the short term for the Joint Soviet-American Statement on Strategic Arms Limitation of November 25, 1974.

116. Aldridge, p. 2893.

117. *Ibid.*, p. 2894.

118. *Ibid.*, p. 2895.

119. *Ibid.*, p. 2896.

120. *Ibid.*, p. 2898.

121. General Russell Dougherty letter to Senator Barry Goldwater, dated February 23, 1976, as entered in the Congressional Record for the hearing on the FY77 Military Procurement Authorization Bill, March 10, 1976, pp. 2831-2832.

122. *Ibid.*

123. *Ibid.*

124. *Ibid.*, p. 2832.

125. Prepared statement of General Russell E. Dougherty, CINCSAC, presented to the Senate Armed Services Committee hearing on the FY77 Military Procurement Authorization Bill, March 10, 1976, p. 2899.

126. General Russell Dougherty letter to Senator Barry Goldwater, dated February 23, 1976, as entered in the Congressional Record for the hearing on the FY77 Military Procurement Authorization Bill, March 10, 1976, pp. 2832.

127. *Ibid.*, pp. 2833-2834.

128. Prepared statement of General Russell E. Dougherty, CINCSAC, presented to the Senate Armed Services Committee hearing on the FY77 Military Procurement Authorization Bill, March 10, 1976, p. 2901.

129. *Ibid.*

130. *Ibid.*, p. 2902.

131. Interview with General Russell E. Dougherty (Ret.), National Security Archive, August 31, 1996, available from *www. gwu.edu/~nsarchiv/coldwar/interviews/episode-12/doughert1.html.*

132. Testimony of General Russell E. Dougherty, CINCSAC, before the Senate Armed Services Committee hearing on the FY77 Military Procurement Authorization Bill, March 10, 1976, p. 2911.

133. Alton H. Quanbeck and Archie L. Wood, *Modernizing the Strategic Bomber Force: Why and How,* Washington, DC: Brookings Institution, 1976, p. 6.

134. Prepared statement of General Russell E. Dougherty, CINCSAC, presented to the Senate Armed Services Committee hearing on the FY77 Military Procurement Authorization Bill, March 10, 1976, p.2903.

135. Quanbeck and Wood, p. 90.

136. Prepared statement of General David C. Jones, Chief of Staff of the Air Force for the Senate Armed Services Committee hearing on the FY77 Military Procurement Authorization bill, March 10, 1976, p. 2869.

137. *Ibid.*, p. 2870.

138. Based on the difficulties in the Poseiden program, many officers argued that missiles could fail for a variety of reasons and the bomber would provide a backup.

139. Prepared statement of General David C. Jones, Chief of Staff of the Air Force for the Senate Armed Services Committee

hearing on the FY77 Military Procurement Authorization Bill, March 10, 1976, p. 2872.

140. *Ibid.*, p. 2875.

141. *Ibid.*, p. 2877.

142. *Ibid.*, p. 2908.

143. *Ibid.*, p. 2909.

144. Interview with former NSC staffer Victor Utgoff, January 26, 2009.

145. NAII, RG340, C/44/4, Box 22 of 34, folder 1854-76, MSN Correspondence Office SAF/CSAF.

146. Archie Wood, "Modernizing the Strategic Bomber Force Without Really Trying-A Case Against the B-1," *International Security*, Vol. 1, No. 2, Autumn 1976, p. 98.

147. Quanbeck and Wood, p. 3.

148. *Ibid.*, p. 19.

149. *Ibid.*, p. 24.

150. *Ibid.*, p. 25.

151. *Ibid.*, p. 26.

152. *Ibid.*, pp. 28-29.

153. *Ibid.* p. 29.

154. *Ibid.*, pp. 31-32.

155. *Ibid.*, p. 33.

156. *Ibid.*

157. *Ibid.*, p. 93.

158. Air Force Studies & Analysis, *Assessment of Quanbeck-Wood Report* presented to the Senate Armed Services Committee, March 10, 1976, pp. 2921-2953.

159. *Ibid.*, p. 2923.

160. *Ibid.*, p. 2927.

161. *Ibid.*, p. 2926.

162. General David C. Jones testimony before the Senate Armed Services Committee, hearing on the FY77 Military Procurement Authorization Bill, March 10, 1976, p. 2912.

163. Air Force Studies & Analysis *Assessment of Quanbeck-Wood Report* presented to the Senate Armed Services Committee, March 10, 1976, p. 2931.

164. *Ibid.*, p. 2937.

165. *Ibid.*, p. 2939.

166. NAII, RG340, C/44/4, Box 22 of 34, folder 1854-76, MSN Correspondence Office SAF/CSAF.

167. Air Force Studies & Analysis *Assessment of Quanbeck-Wood Report* presented to the Senate Armed Services Committee, March 10, 1976, p. 2945.

168. Nicholas Wade, "Death of the B-1: The Events Behind Carter's Decision," *Science*, Vol. 197, No. 4303, August 5, 1977, p. 536.

169. *Ibid.*, p. 537.

170. *Ibid.*

171. Author interview with Dr. Harold Brown, February 2, 2009.

172. Author interview with former NSC staffer Victor Utgoff, January 16, 2009.

173. "Carter's Big Decision: Down Goes the B-1, Here Comes the Cruise," *Time* July 11, 1977, available from *www.time.com/time/printout/0,8816,919040,00.html*.

174. Jimmy Carter, *Keeping Faith: Memoirs of a President*, New York: Bantam Books, 1982, p. 82.

175. Author interview with former NSC staffer Victor Utgoff, January 16, 2009.

176. Interview with former Secretary of Defense Harold Brown, February 2, 2009.

177. For the B-1, B-52, and FB-111A radar cross sections, see Dennis R. Jenkins, *B-1 Lancer: The Most Complicated Warplane Ever Developed*, New York: McGraw Hill, 1999, p. 48.

178. Carter, pp. 81-83.

179. "Carter's Big Decision."

180. *Ibid.*

181. *Ibid.*

182. Quoted in Erik B. Riker-Coleman, *Political Pressures on the Joint Chiefs of Staff: The Case of General David C. Jones*, 2001, available from *www.unc.edu/~chaos1/jones.pdf*.

183. Caspar W. Weinberger, *Fighting for Peace: Seven Critical Years in the Pentagon*, New York: Warner Books, 1990, p. 48.

184. This is not the place to debate whether Carter's policies contributed or detracted from national security; it suffices that the Republicans believed they had. Even today among Air Force officers there is residual belief that Carter weakened defense and the B-1 is the primary example used to demonstrate this.

185. Weinberger, *Fighting for Peace*, p. 43.

186. Jenkins, p. 61.

187. Caspar W. Weinberger, *Department of Defense Annual Report to the Congress for Fiscal Year 1983*, Washington, DC: Government Printing Office, February 8, 1982, p. I-41.

188. *Ibid.*, p. IV-3.

189. Jenkins, p. xiii.

190. Author interview with Dr Harold Brown, February 2, 2009.

191. The B-1 has provided some close air support in Afghanistan and Iraq using conventional munitions.

192. Interview by the author with an anonymous senior defense official.

193. *Ibid.*

194. George W. Bush, "A Period of Consequences," speech at the Citadel, September 23, 1999, available from *www.citadel.edu/pao.addresses/pres_bush.html*.

195. *Ibid.*

196. Tom Mullins, Tom White interviews.

197. "Gov. Bush and Defense," *The Washington Post*, Editorial, September 26, 1999, p. B06.

198. Rowan Scarborough, "Bush Proposes Military Changes; Futuristic Weapons, Land Forces on List," *The Washington Times*, September 24, 1999, p. A1.

199. CNN interview from January 26, 2000, quoted by John Cochran, *World News Tonight*, ABC News, April 22, 2002.

200. Army Chief of Staff General Eric K. Shinseki's Address to the Eisenhower Luncheon, 45th Annual Meeting of the Association of the United States Army, October 12, 1999.

201. *Ibid.*

202. Eric K. Shinseki, "Beginning the Next 100 Years," *Army*, October 1999, p.28.

203. Edward F. Bruner and Steve Bowman, "Crusader XM2001 Self-Propelled Howitzer: Background and Issues for Congress," RS21218, Washington, DC: Congressional Research Service, Updated June 25, 2002.

204. Author interview with Tom Mullins, DASA, February 17, 2009.

205. Author Interviews with Tom Mullins, February 17, 2009; and Lieutenant Colonel (Ret.) Jan Jedrych, former member of Army G-4, January 26, 2009.

206. Author interview with Tom Mullins, February 17, 2009.

207. Author interviews with Tom Mullins and Jan Jedrych.

208. John M. Matsumura *et al.*, *Assessment of Crusader: The Army's Next Self-Propelled Howitzer and Resupply Vehicle*, Santa Monica, CA: RAND, 1998, p. iii.

209. *Ibid.*, p. xi.

210. *Ibid.*, p. 2.

211. *Ibid.*, pp. 3-4.

212. *Ibid.*, pp. 30, 37.

213. *Ibid.*, p. 22.

214. *Ibid.*, p. 14.

215. Author interview with Tom Mullins, February 17, 2009.

216. Author interviews with several OSD and Army officials brought up this theory, but few people were willing to admit they believed this was the case.

217. PR Newswire, "Crusader SPH1 Prototype Successfully Completes 60-Round Fire-Through Confidence Test," February 1, 2000.

218. Robert Burns, "Army Secretary Holds Out Possibility of Criminal Prosecutions," *The Associated Press*, February 2, 2000.

219. Louis Caldera testimony before the Senate Armed Services Committee on the FY2001 Defense Budget, February 10, 2000.

220. *Ibid*.

221. "US Senator John Warner (R-VA) Holds Hearing with the Service Secretaries," *FDCH Political Transcripts*, February 10, 2000.

222. Steven Lee Myers, "Bush Candidate for Defense Job Sees Overhaul," *The New York Times*, January 12, 2001, p. A1.

223. *Ibid*.

224. *Ibid*., p. A15.

225. Author interview with former senior DoD officials.

226. Author interview with Barry Watts, Jaymie Durnan, Christopher Lamb, and Michael Wynne. Thom Shanker and James Dao, "Defense Secretary Wants Cuts in Weapons Systems to Pay for New Technologies," *The New York Times*, April 16, 2002, p. A25.

227. Shanker and Dao, p. A25.

228. Author conversation with OSD Policy official, May 2001.

229. "Pentagon Panel Recommends Canceling New Artillery System," *Associated Press*, April 23, 2001.

230. Pauline Jelinek, "Military Braces for Rumsfeld Recommendation," *Associated Press*, April 23, 2001.

231. "Watts not Giving up on Defense Plan," *Associated Press State & Local Wire*, April 23, 2001.

232. Author interview with former Deputy Secretary of Defense Paul D. Wolfowitz, February 23, 2009.

233. OSD official's meeting notes from May 8, 2001.

234. Rowan Scarborough, "Pentagon Staff to be Trimmed by 15 Percent; Bureaucracy an Adversary, Rumsfeld says," *The Washington Times*, September 11, 2001, p. A1.

235. Author interview with former Secretary of the Army Thomas White, January 23, 2009.

236. Author interview with former Deputy Secretary of Defense Paul D. Wolfowitz, February 23, 2009.

237. Robert Borosage, "Rumsfeld's Surrender," *The Washington Post*, February 7, 2002, p. A25.

238. "U.S. Senator Daniel Inouye (D-HI) Holds Hearing on FY-2003 Army Appropriations," *FDCH Political Transcripts*, March 6, 2002.

239. *Ibid.*

240. *Ibid.*

241. Paul D. Wolfowitz testimony before the Senate Armed Services Committee hearing on Defense Needs in the 21st Century, April 9, 2002.

242. *Ibid.*

243. Author interviews with Ray DuBois, Jaymie Durnan, and Barry Watts.

244. Unclassified "Action Memo," Subject: Crusader Analysis from Barry Watts to Deputy Secretary Wolfowitz, dated April 24, 2002.

245. Barry Watts notes from meeting: Wolfowitz emphasized his desire to keep the funding in Army programs to ensure the Army continued to benefit from the research; author interview with Paul Wolfowitz on February 23, 2009. Of note, several participants in the process from both OSD and the Army argued that they were pivotal to ensuring that the funding remained in Army programs.

246. Author interview with Jaymie Durnan, January 13, 2009, and Ray DuBois, February 17, 2009.

247. Author interview with former Deputy Secretary of Defense Paul D. Wolfowitz, February 23, 2009.

248. Author interview with Ray DuBois, February 17, 2009.

249. Author interview with Jaymie Durnan, January 13, 2009.

250. Barry Watts notes from May 1, 2002.

251. Author interview with Ray DuBois, February 17, 2009; and Barry Watts notes from May 1, 2002.

252. Author interview with senior DoD official.

253. Author interview with Tom Mullins. J. C. Watts, the Oklahoma Congressman, was particularly angered by the way the administration handled the decision.

254. Hearing before the Senate Armed Services Committee, "The Crusader Artillery System," S. Hrg 107-804, May 16, 2002, 2nd Sess., p. 12.

255. *Ibid.*, p. 3.

256. *Ibid.*, pp. 17, 19.

257. *Ibid.*, p. 20.

258. *Ibid.*, p. 23.

259. *Ibid.*, p. 87.

260. *Ibid.*, p. 92.

261. Author interview with several field-grade officers involved in the Crusader program.

262. Author interview with Ian Jedrych, January 26, 2009.

263. Andrew F. Krepinevich, testimony before the Senate Armed Services Committee hearing on Meeting Defense Needs of the 21st Century, April 9, 2002.

264. Author interviews with former Director, Program Analysis & Evaluation, Barry Watts and former Director, Land Forces Division in PA&E, Mark Cancian.

265. Author interviews with former Secretary of the Army Thomas White, and senior Army official Tom Mullins.

266. Author interviews with former Deputy Secretary Paul Wolfowitz and Army senior official Tom Mullins.

267. Author interview with Jaymie Durnan, January 13, 2009.

268. Author interview with former DASD for Resources and Plans Christopher Lamb, December 11, 2008.

269. Author interviews with senior OSD officials.

270. Enthoven, p. 6.

271. For more on this thought, see Carl H. Builder, *The Masks of War: American Military Styles in Strategy and Analysis*, Baltimore, MD: Johns Hopkins University Press, 1989.

272. Hayward and Borklund, p. 276.

273. Fenella McGerty, "Gates Calls for Clampdown on Leaks of Budget Details," *Jane's Defence Weekly*, March 4, 2009, p. 10; and Greg Jaffe and Shailagh Murray, "Gates Seeks Sharp Turn in Spending; Defense Budget Focuses on Lower-Tech Weapons," *The Washington Post*, April 7, 2009, p. A1.

274. Interview with Ray DuBois, February 17, 2009.

275. Chris Cillizza, "Obama Picks GOP Rep. McHugh To Be His Secretary of the Army," *The Washington Post*, June 3, 2009, p. A3.

276. Kara Rowland, "Democrats Stand Up for Home-State Facilities; Budget Cuts Hit Too Close for Comfort," *The Washington Times*, April 14, 2009, p. A6; and "Dodd Rallies to Union's Side to Oppose F-22 Budget Cuts" *FOXNews*, April 9, 2009, available from *www.foxnews.com/politics/2009/04/09/dodd-caught-crossfire-calls-halt-f-production/*. It appears that President Obama and Secretary Gates have won the F-22 debate by wielding the veto threat credibly, but it is a blunt tool that cannot be used in every case. Christopher Drew, "Obama wins crucial round in Senate vote on F-22," *New York Times*, July 22, 2009, p. A1.

277. The Obama administration plans on budgeting for ongoing operations in Iraq and Afghanistan through the regular budget starting with the FY2010 budget, making the FY2009 supplemental the last planned request of its kind.